THE DOOMED SPIRIT OF
LA LLORONA
A GHOSTLY GRAPHIC

by Nel Yomtov
illustrated by Jason Millet

CAPSTONE PRESS
a capstone imprint

Published by Capstone Press, an imprint of Capstone
1710 Roe Crest Drive, North Mankato, Minnesota 56003
capstonepub.com

Library of Congress Cataloging-in-Publication Data
Names: Yomtov, Nel, author. | Millet, Jason, illustrator.
Title: The doomed spirit of La Llorona : a ghostly graphic /
by Nel Yomtov; illustrated by Jason Millet.
Description: North Mankato, Minnesota : Capstone Press, 2024. | Series:
Ghostly graphics | Includes bibliographical references. | Audience: Ages
9 to 11 | Audience: Grades 4–6 | Summary: "The Latin American tale of
La Llorona strikes fear in the hearts of all who hear it. It begins with a woman
who drowns her children in a fit of rage and jealously. It ends with a weeping
specter rumored to pull anyone she encounters to a watery grave. Where did
the legend of this murderous mother begin? And why is La Llorona doomed to
wander the waterways for all eternity? Young readers will find out in this
easy-to-read ghostly graphic novel that will send shivers down their spines!"
—Provided by publisher.
Identifiers: LCCN 2022047857 (print) | LCCN 2022047858 (ebook) |
ISBN 9781669050728 (hardcover) | ISBN 9781669071327 (paperback) | ISBN
9781669050681 (pdf) | ISBN 9781669050704 (kindle edition) |
ISBN 9781669050711 (epub)
Subjects: LCSH: Llorona (Legendary character)—Comic books, strips, etc. |
Legends—Latin America—Comic books, strips, etc. | LCGFT: Graphic novels
Classification: LCC GR114 .Y66 2024 (print) | LCC GR114 (ebook) | DDC
398.25098—dc23/eng/20221208
LC record available at https://lccn.loc.gov/2022047857
LC ebook record available at https://lccn.loc.gov/2022047858

Editorial Credits
Editor: Christopher Harbo; Designer: Tracy Davies;
Production Specialist: Katy LaVigne

All internet sites appearing in back matter were available and accurate when
this book was sent to press.

Printed and bound in the USA. 5425

TABLE OF CONTENTS

INTRODUCTION

LATIN AMERICA'S GHASTLY GHOULS AND GHOSTS

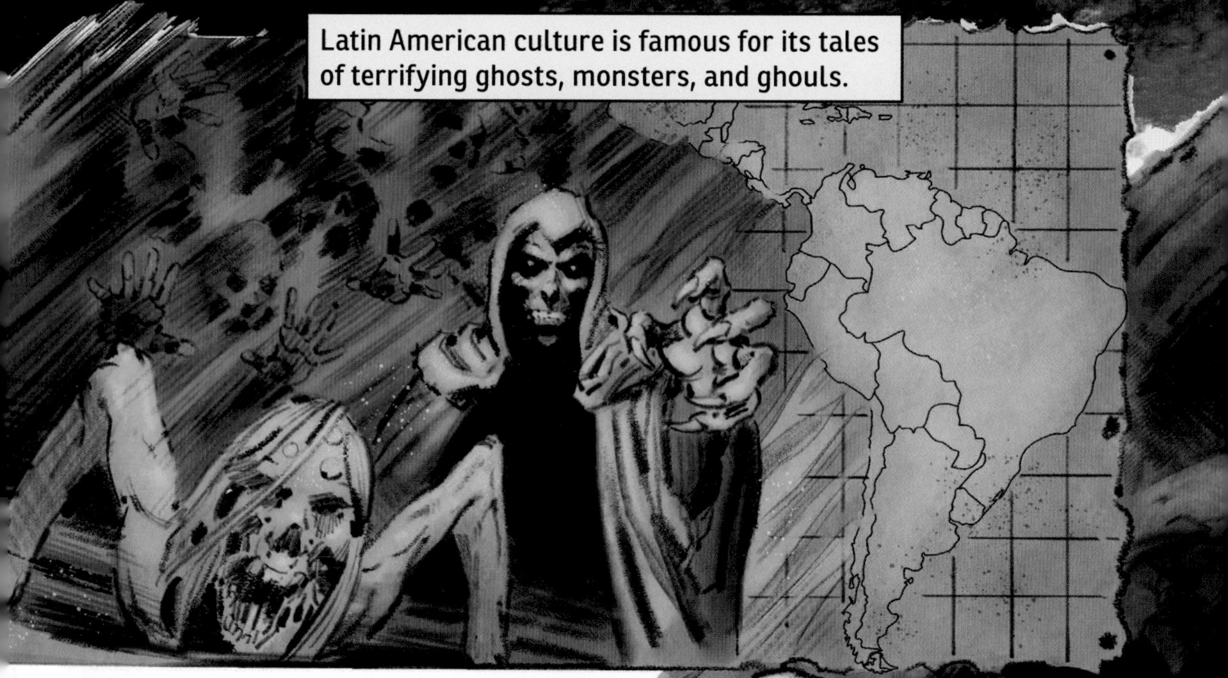
Latin American culture is famous for its tales of terrifying ghosts, monsters, and ghouls.

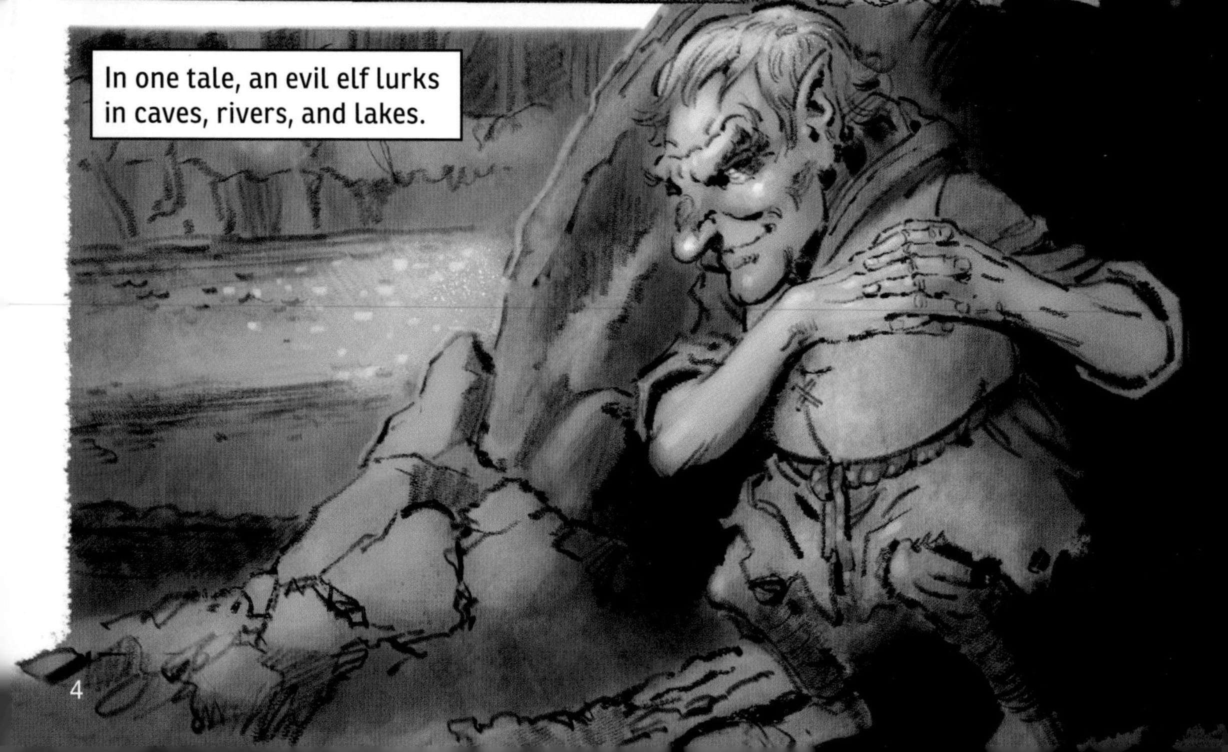
In one tale, an evil elf lurks in caves, rivers, and lakes.

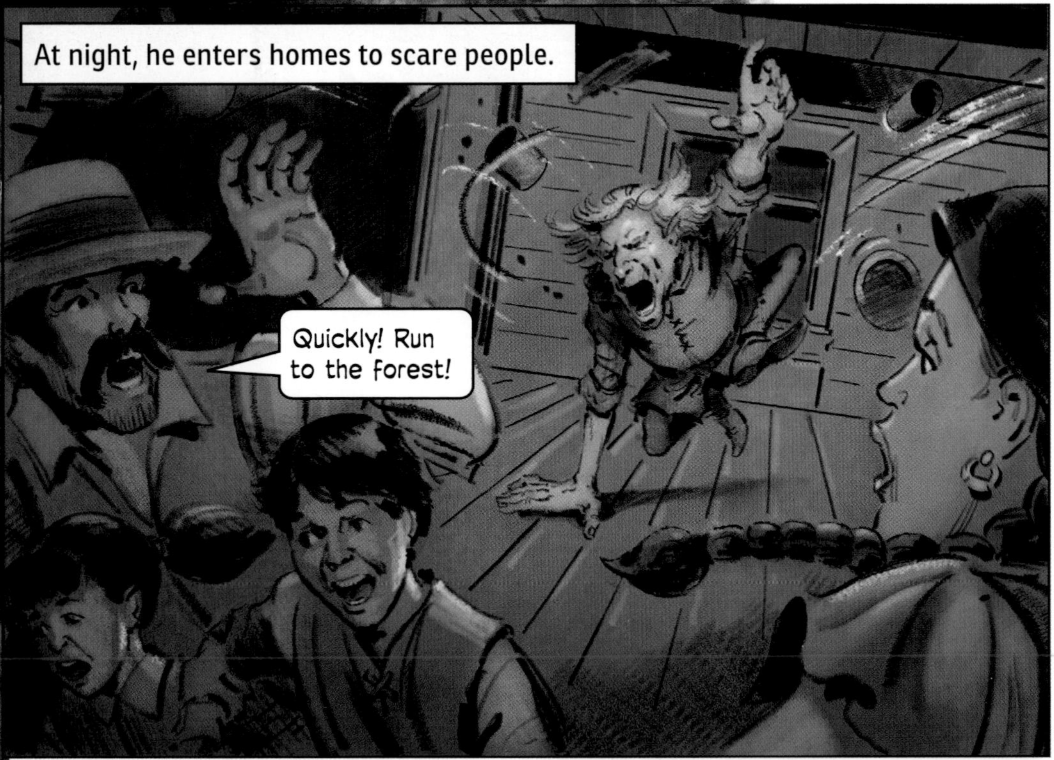
At night, he enters homes to scare people.
Quickly! Run to the forest!

In Chile, tales are told of a shape-shifting vampire.

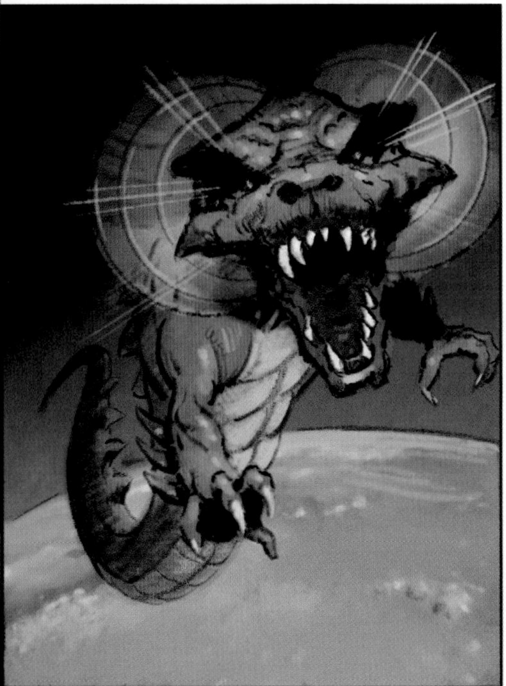

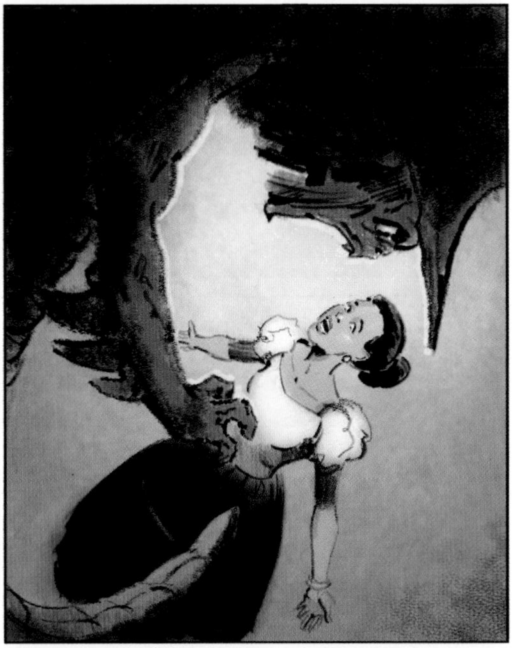

The evil creature puts people into a trance. Then he steals their souls or drains their bodies of blood.

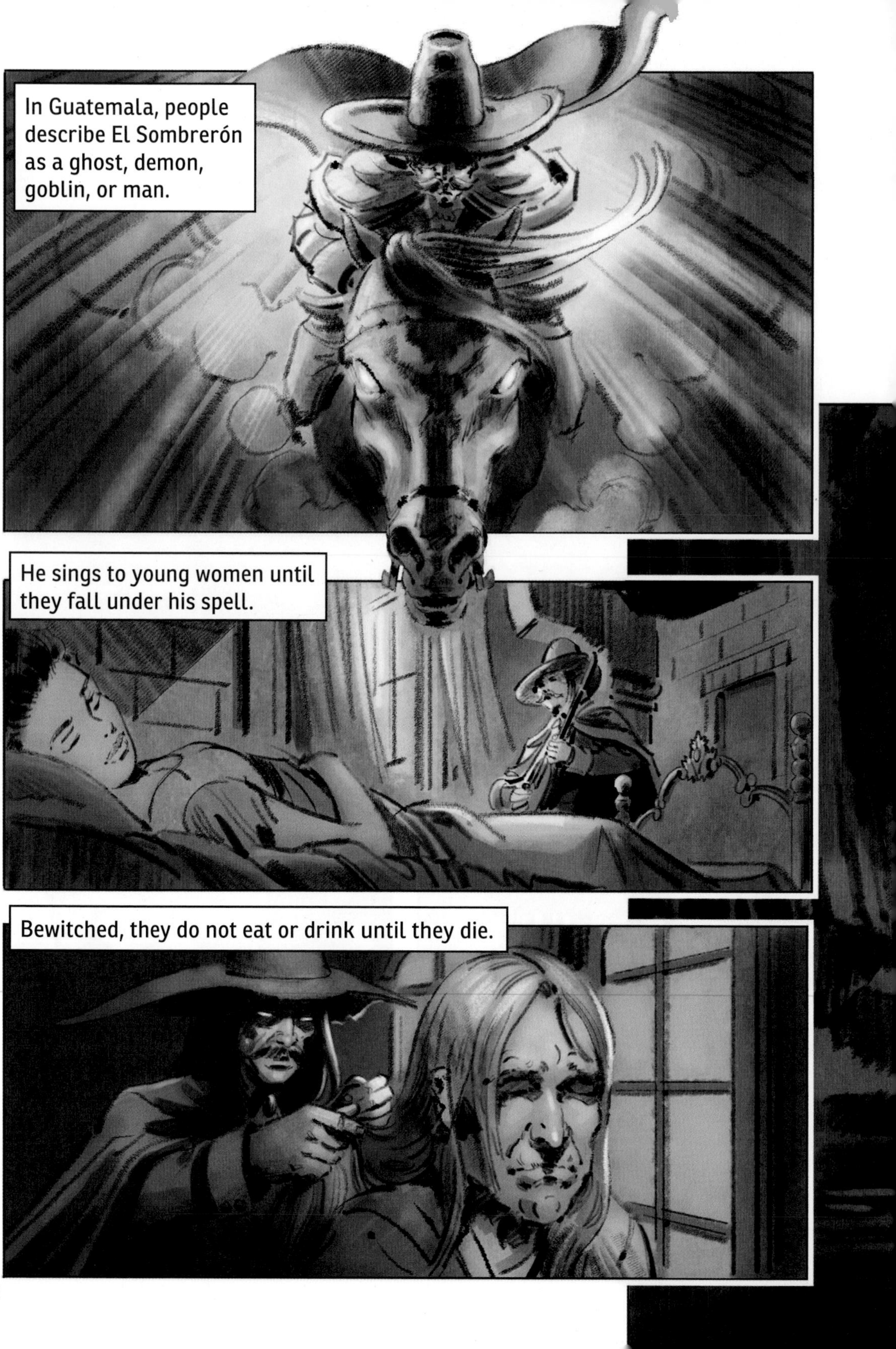
In Guatemala, people describe El Sombrerón as a ghost, demon, goblin, or man.
He sings to young women until they fall under his spell.
Bewitched, they do not eat or drink until they die.

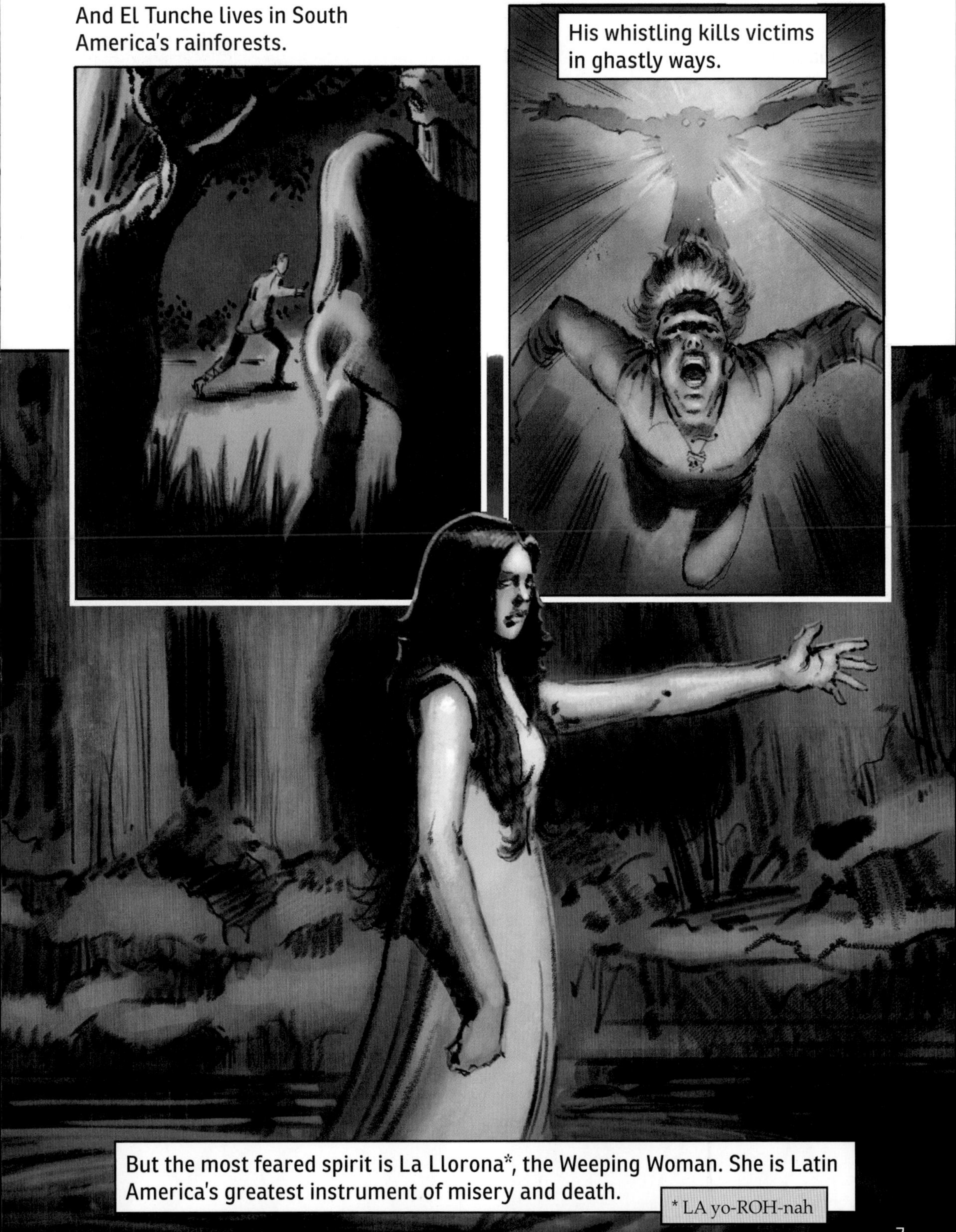
And El Tunche lives in South America's rainforests.
His whistling kills victims in ghastly ways.
But the most feared spirit is La Llorona*, the Weeping Woman. She is Latin America's greatest instrument of misery and death.
* LA yo-ROH-nah

CHAPTER 1

LA LLORONA: THE WEEPING WOMAN

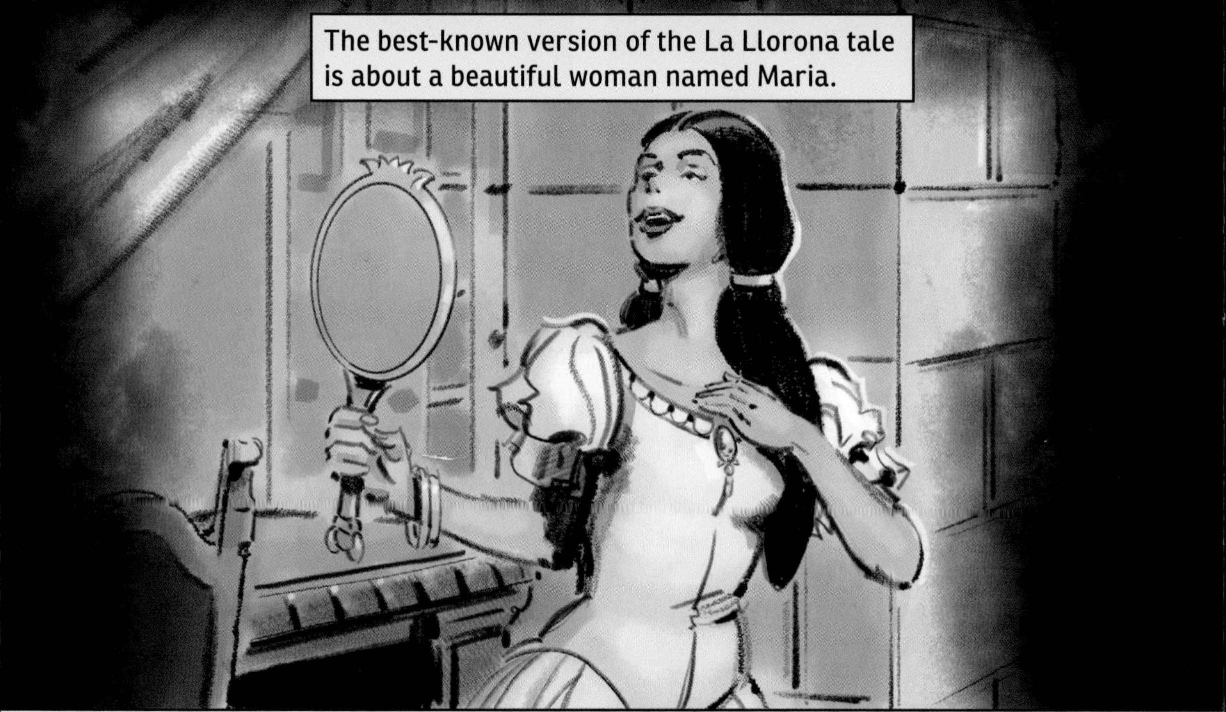
The best-known version of the La Llorona tale is about a beautiful woman named Maria.

Maria was so beautiful she thought no man in town was good enough to marry her.

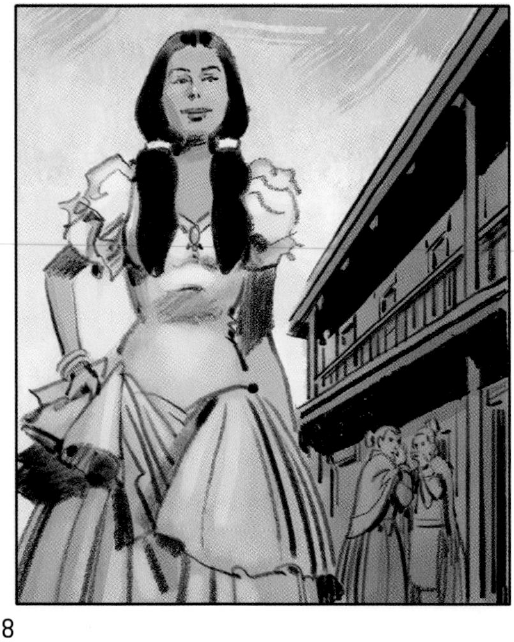

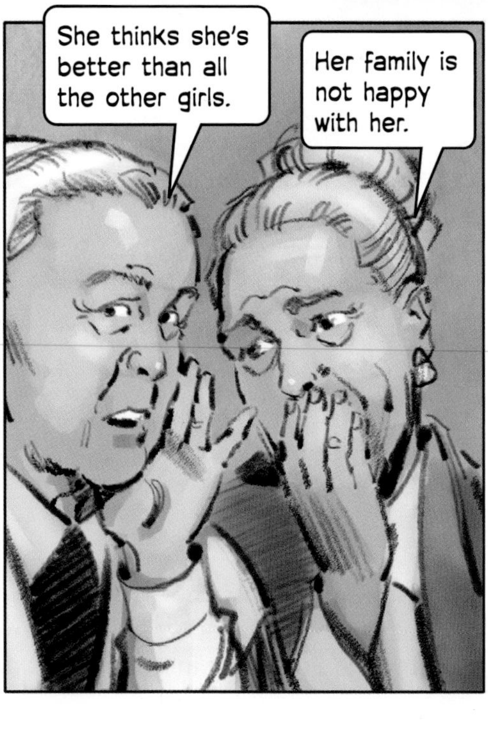
She thinks she's better than all the other girls.
Her family is not happy with her.

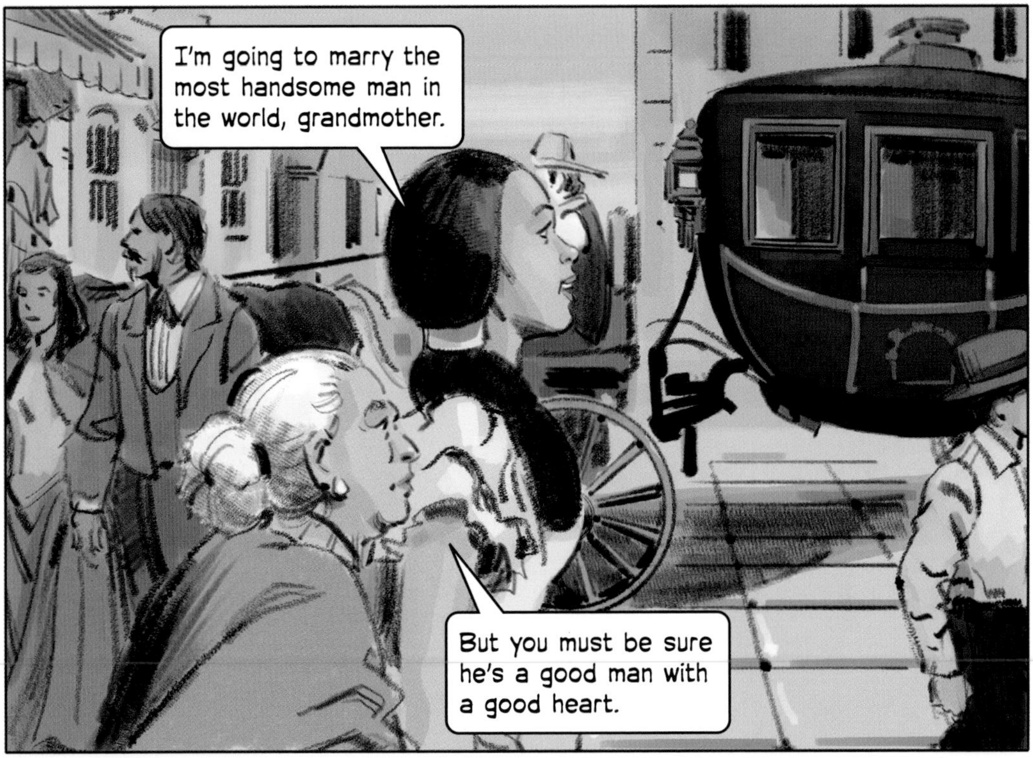
I'm going to marry the most handsome man in the world, grandmother.
But you must be sure he's a good man with a good heart.

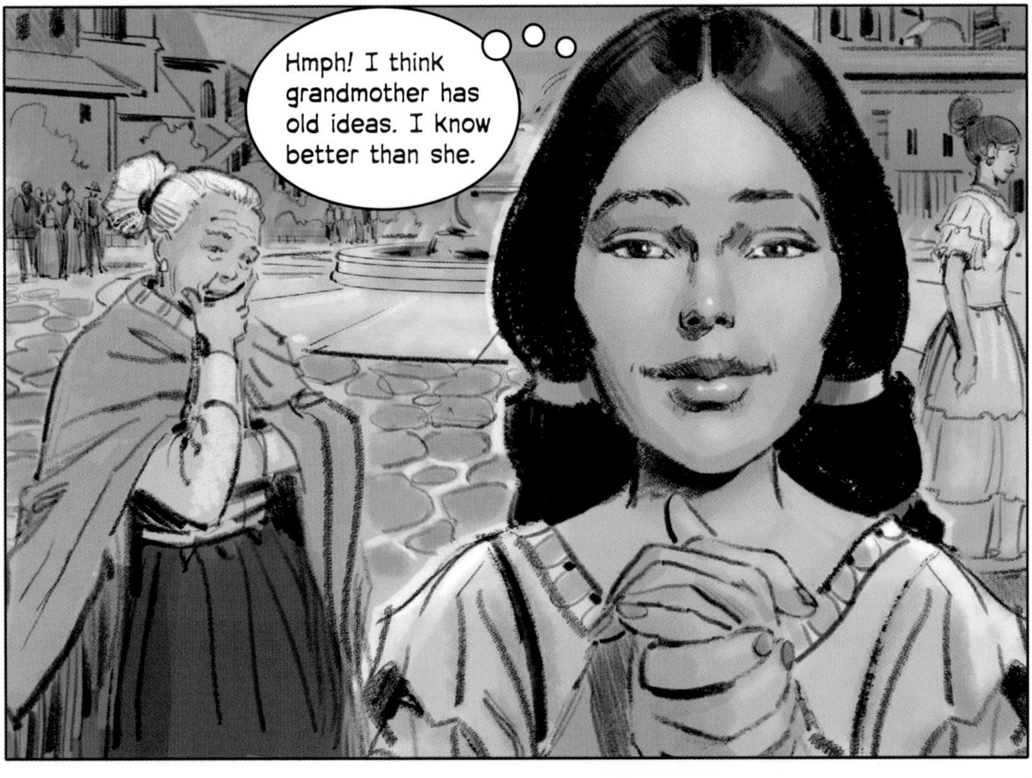
Hmph! I think grandmother has old ideas. I know better than she.

One day, a handsome cowboy came to town.
He was the kind of man Maria dreamed about.

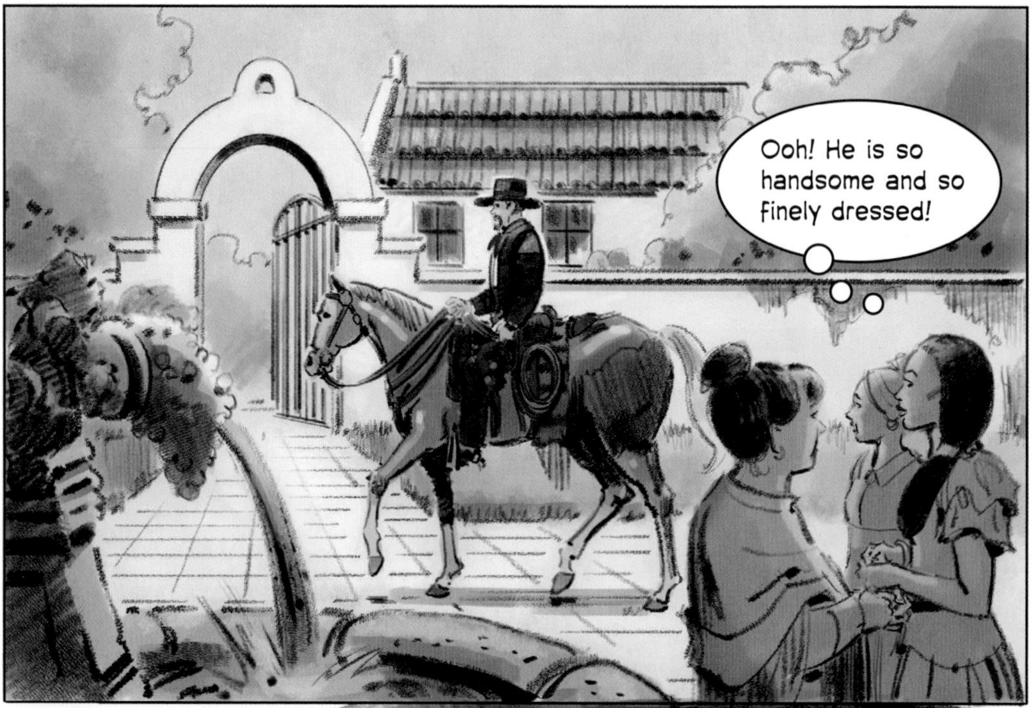
Ooh! He is so handsome and so finely dressed!

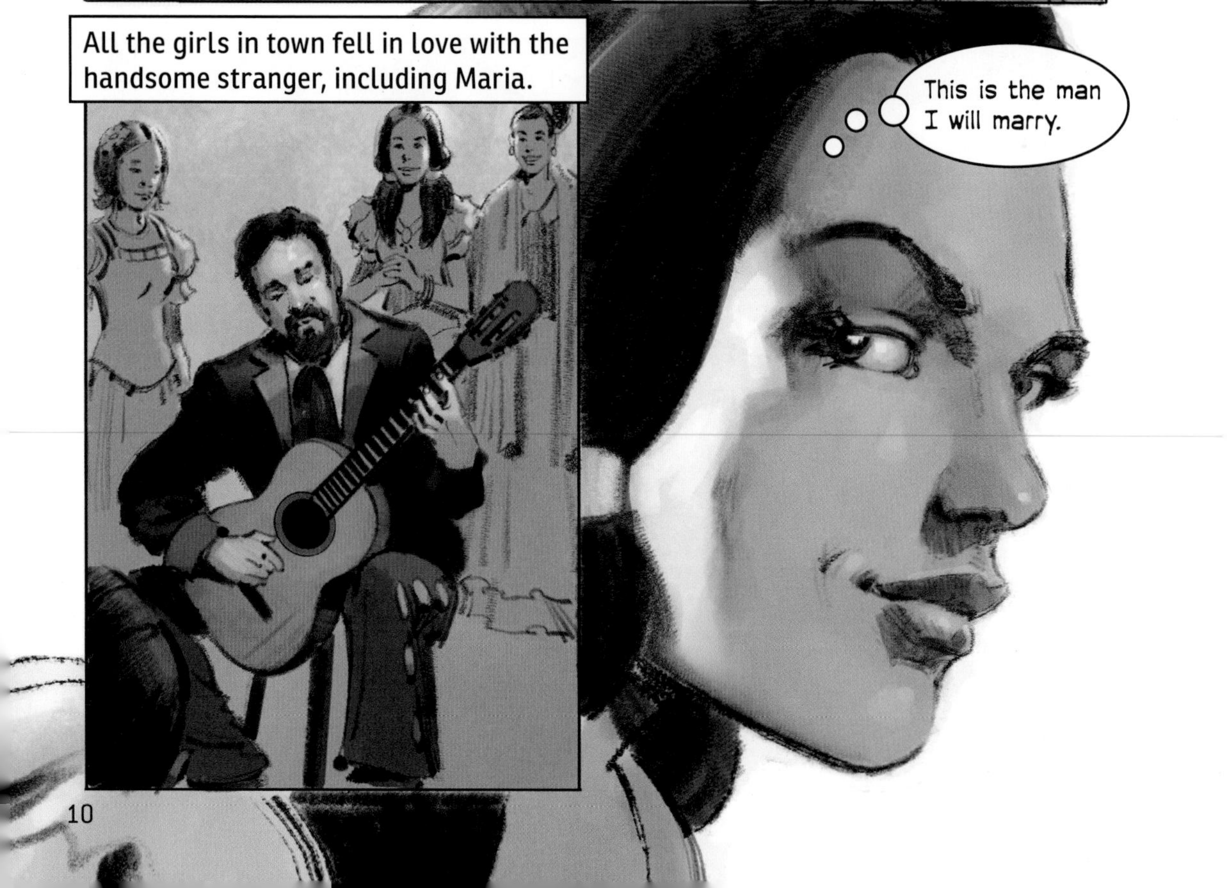
All the girls in town fell in love with the handsome stranger, including Maria.
This is the man I will marry.

The cowboy was attracted to Maria. He made up his mind to marry her.

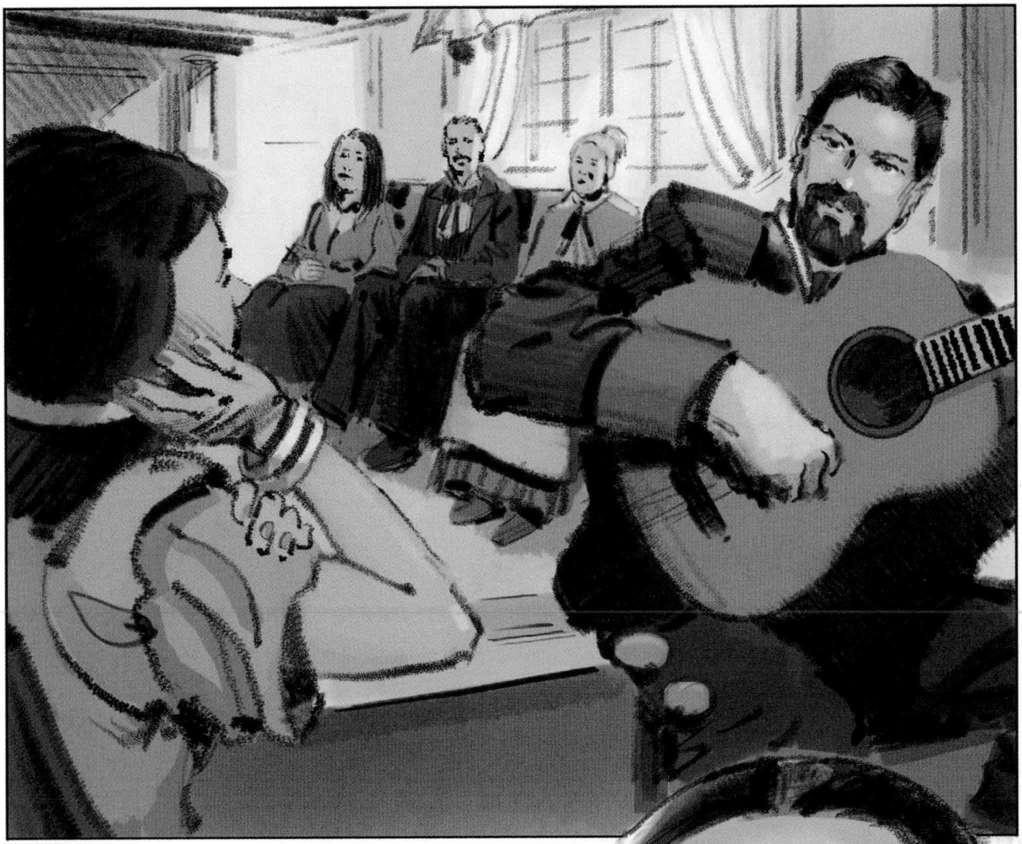

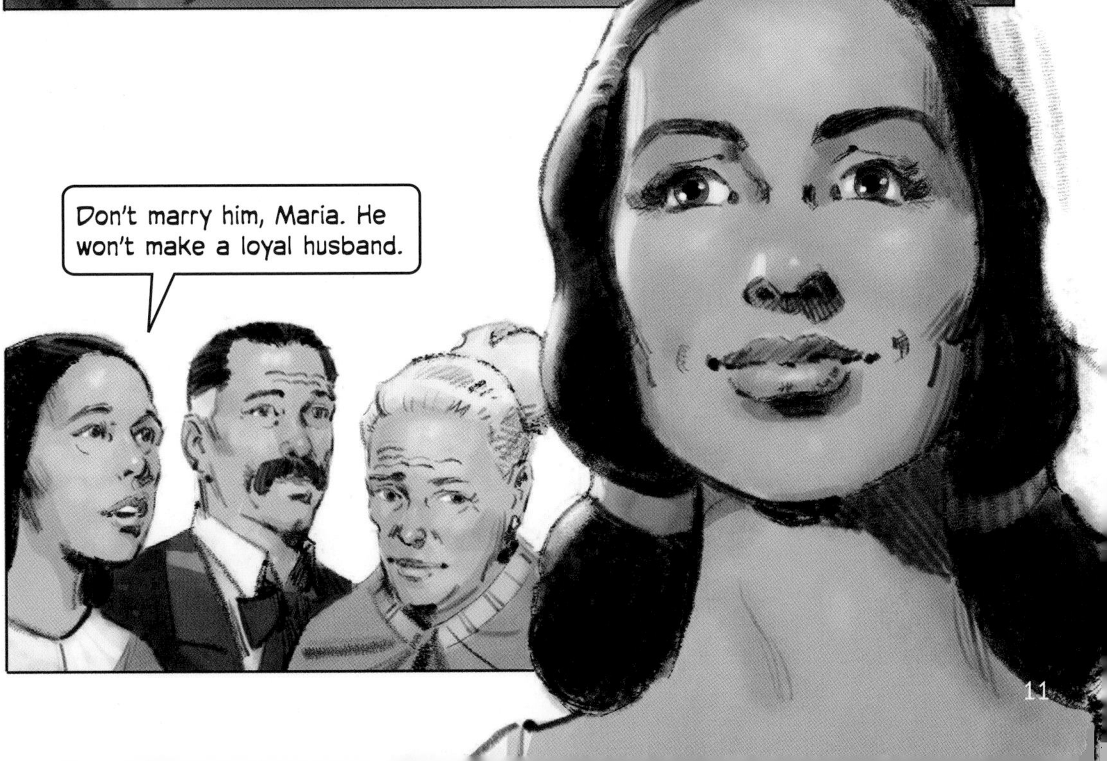
Don't marry him, Maria. He won't make a loyal husband.

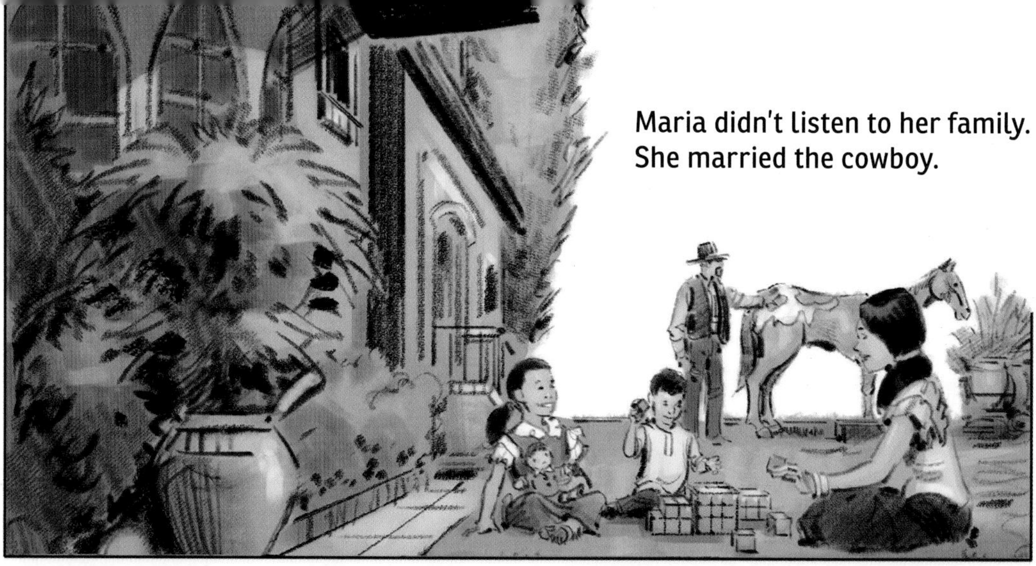
Maria didn't listen to her family.
She married the cowboy.

The couple had two children and a fine home. The family seemed very happy.

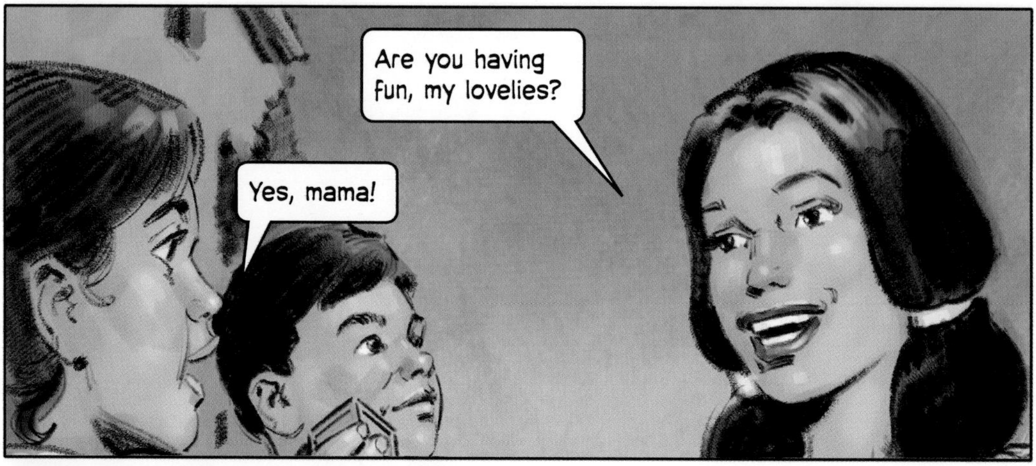
Are you having fun, my lovelies?
Yes, mama!

After a while, Maria's husband would leave town for months at a time.

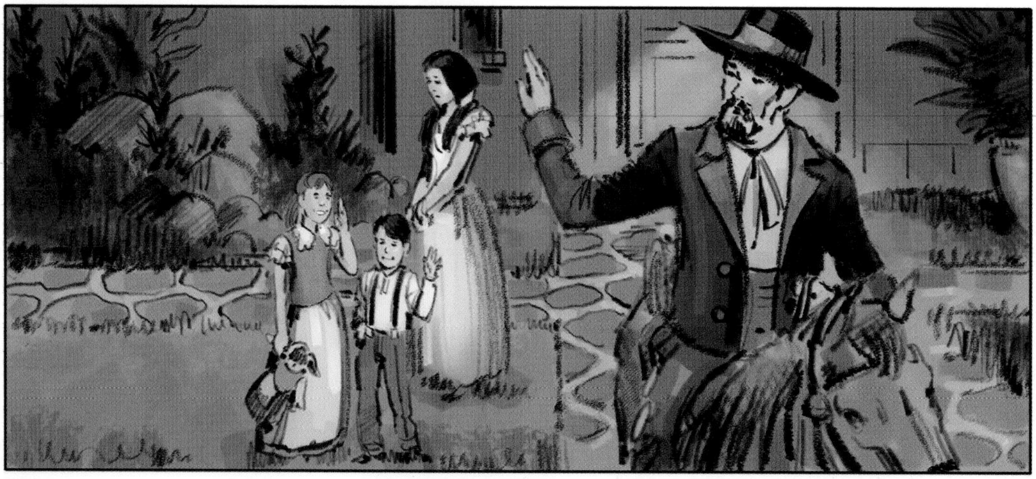

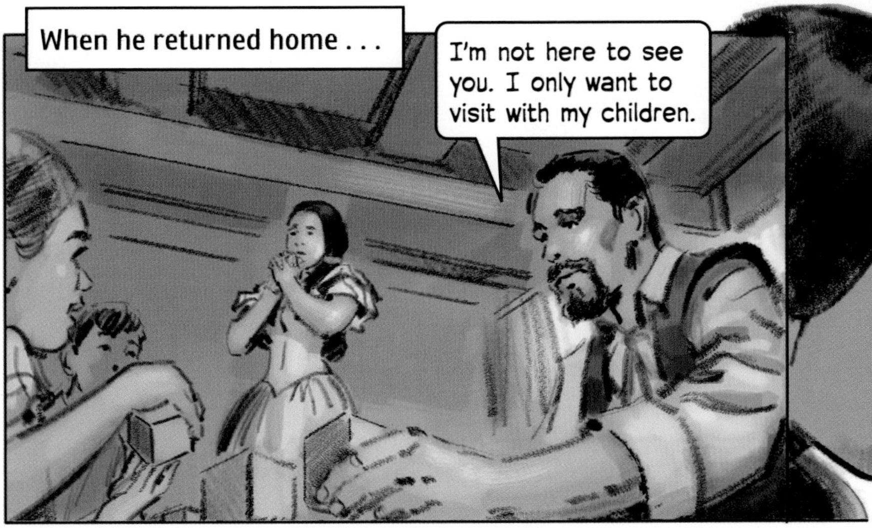
When he returned home . . .
I'm not here to see you. I only want to visit with my children.

Then one night . . .

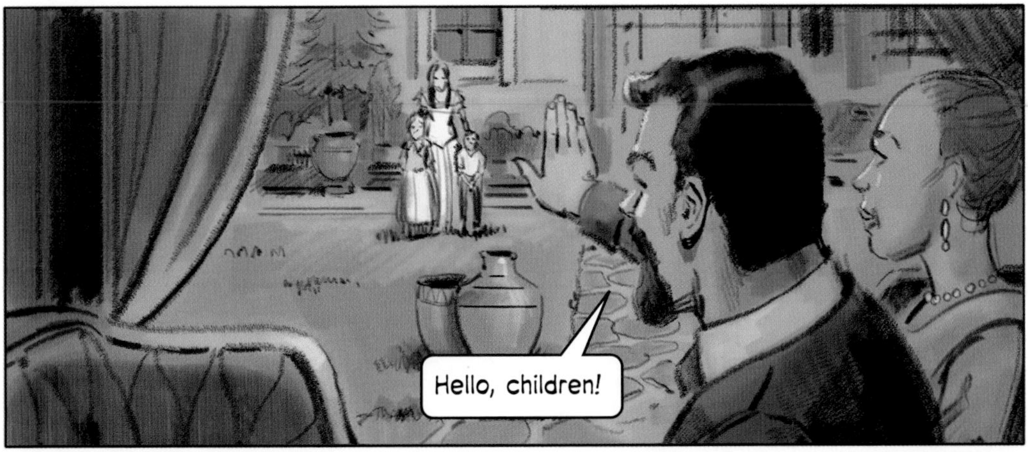
Hello, children!

Maria's husband arrived with another woman. Maria became angry and jealous.

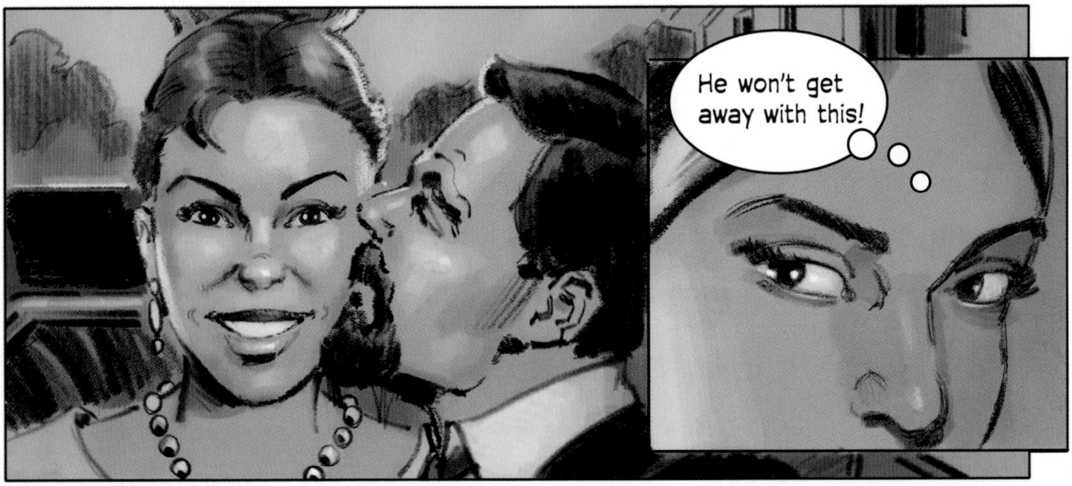
He won't get away with this!

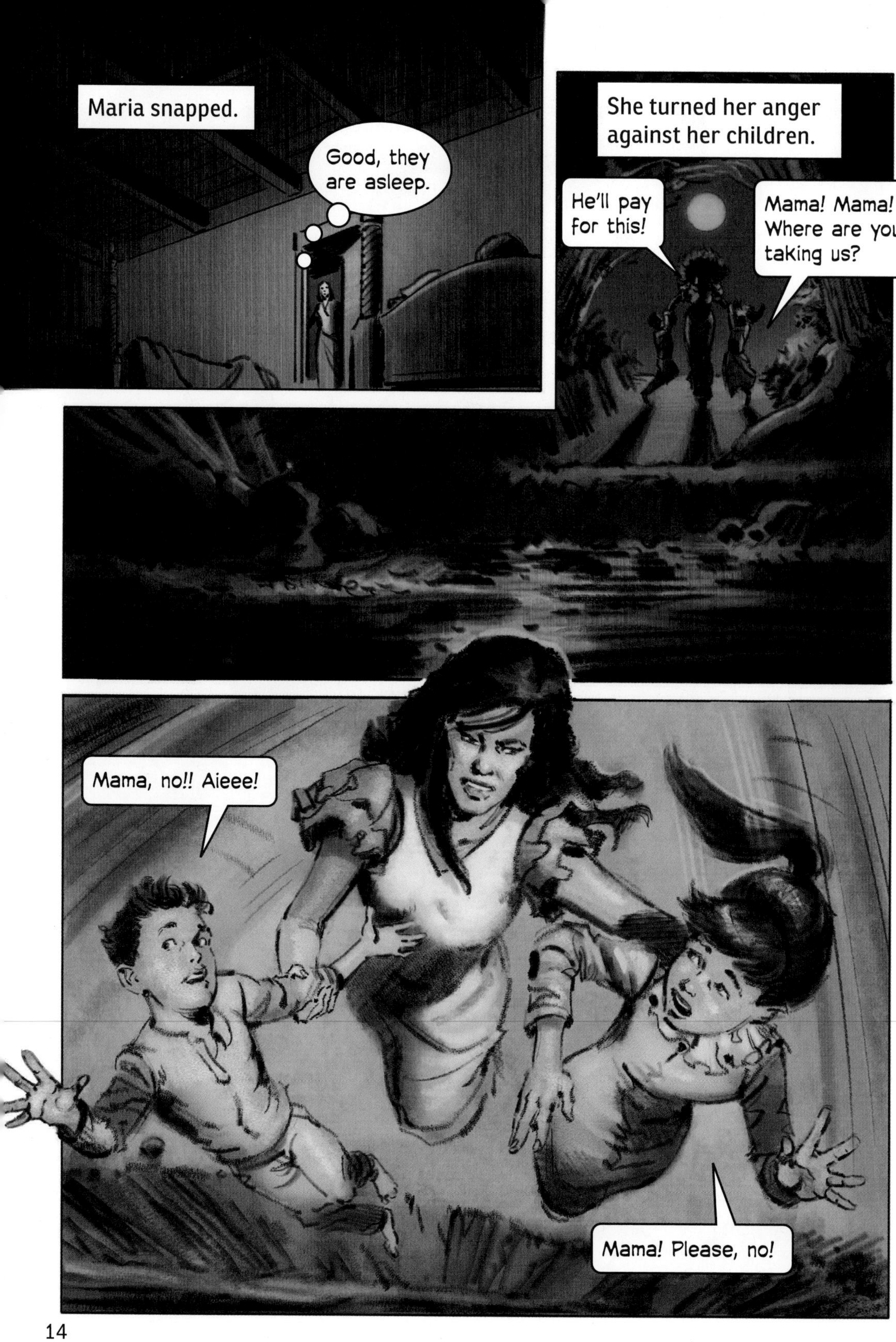
Maria snapped.
Good, they are asleep.
She turned her anger against her children.
He'll pay for this!
Mama! Mama! Where are you taking us?
Mama, no!! Aieee!
Mama! Please, no!

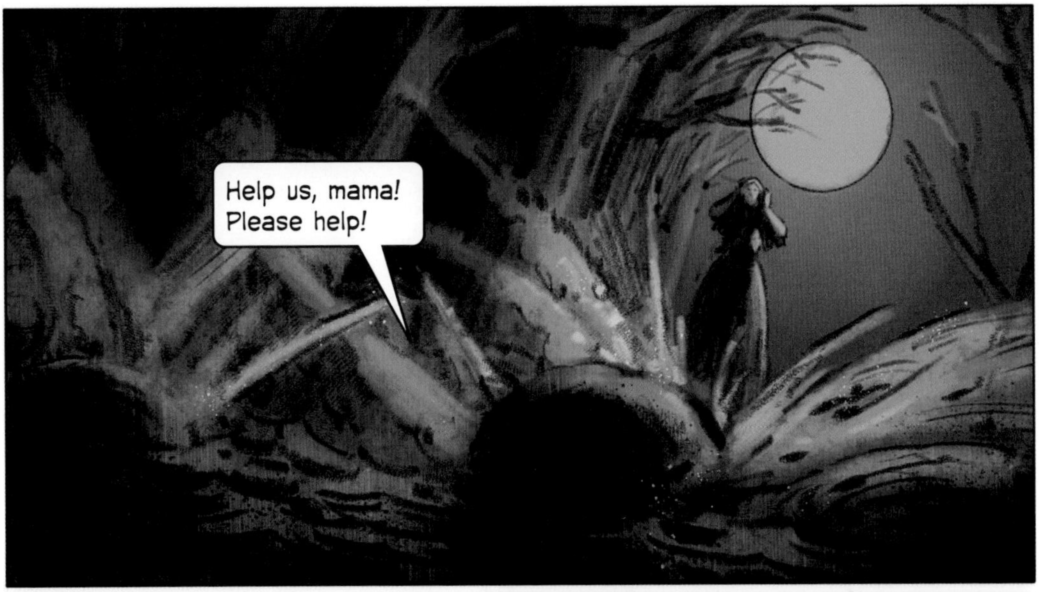
Help us, mama!
Please help!

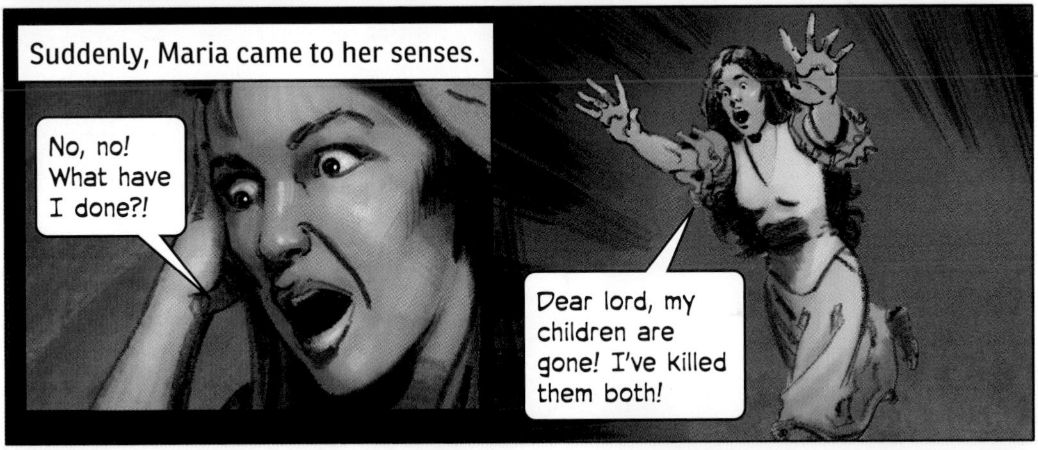
Suddenly, Maria came to her senses.
No, no! What have I done?!
Dear lord, my children are gone! I've killed them both!

Maria didn't notice a large rock along the river.

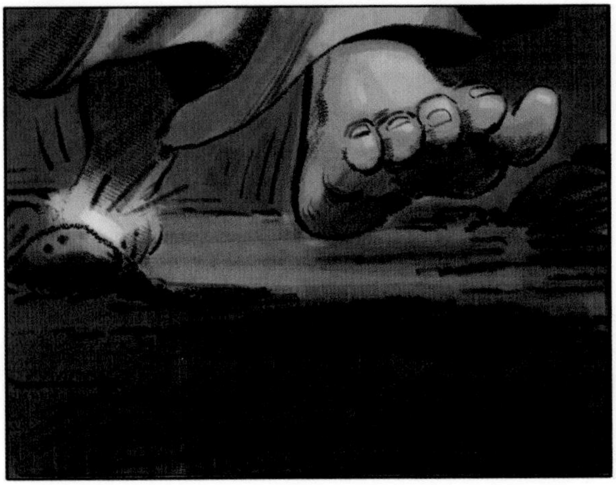

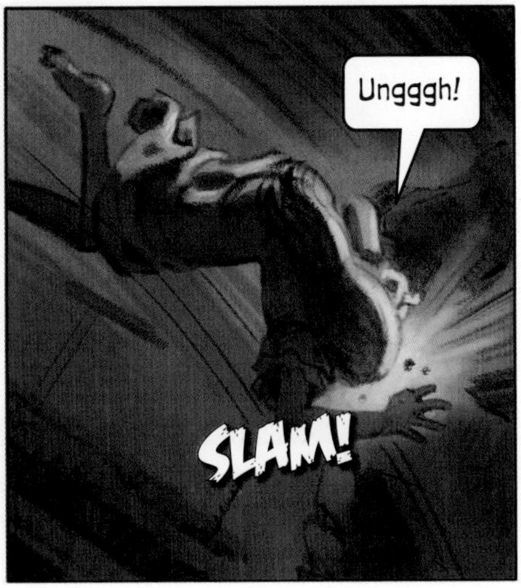
Ungggh!
SLAM!

Maria's fall killed her. The next day she was buried near the river.

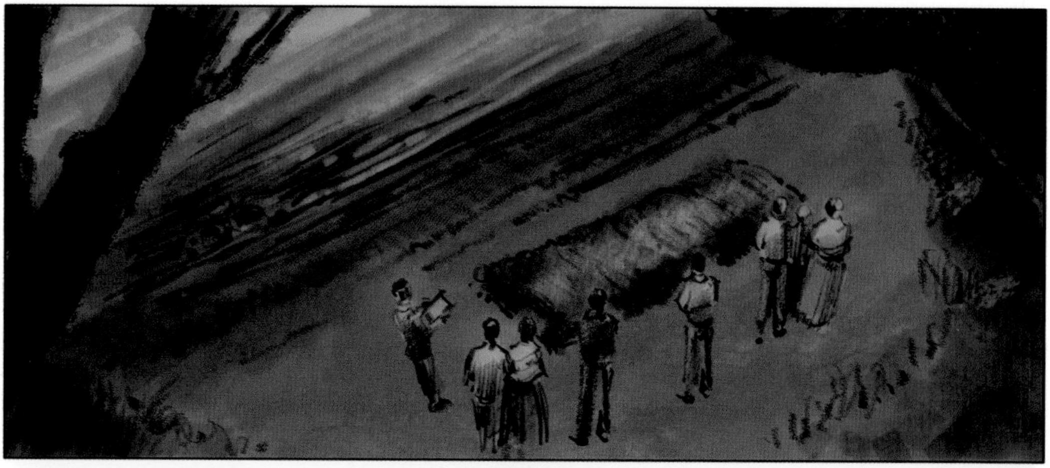

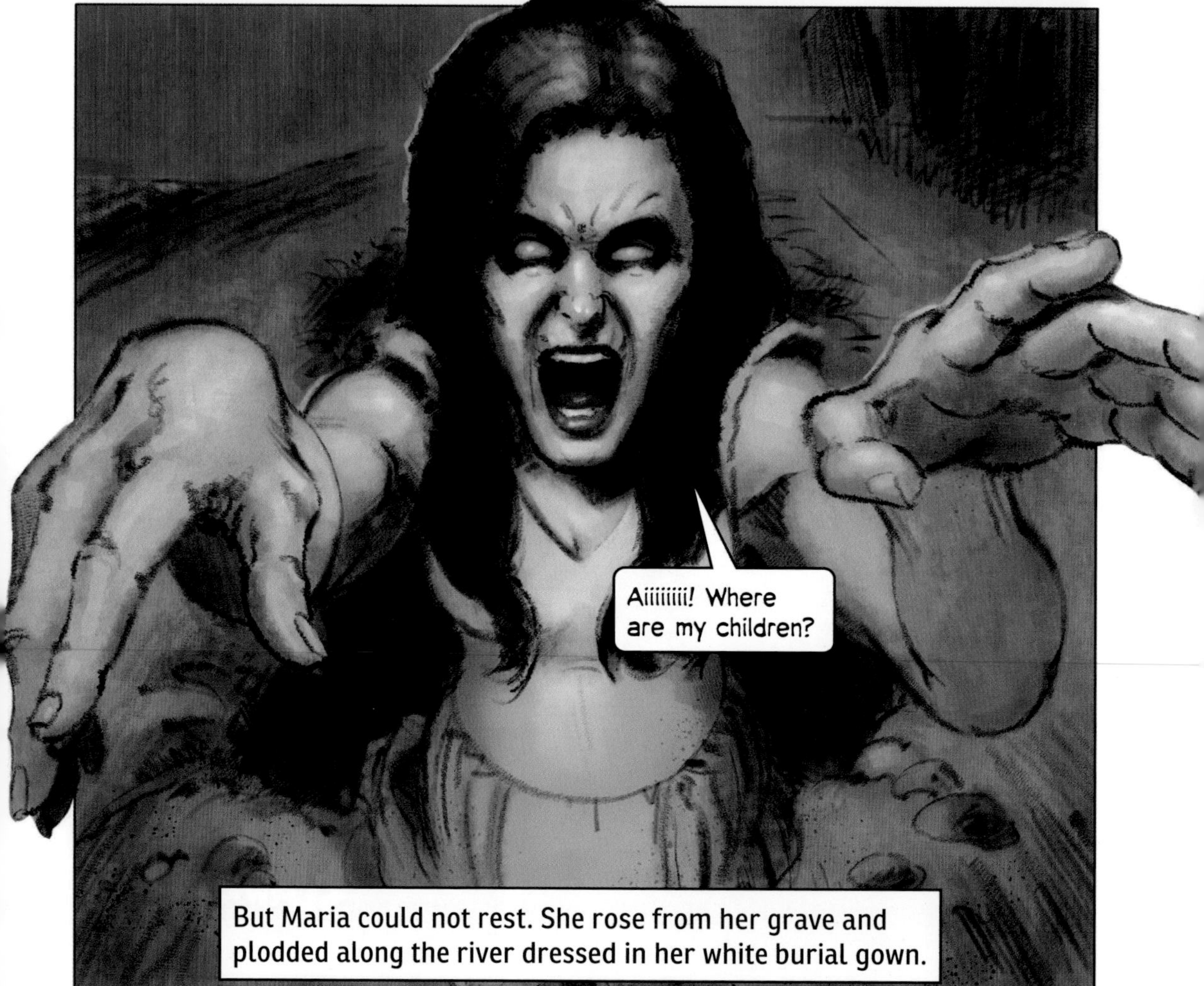
Aiiiiiii! Where are my children?
But Maria could not rest. She rose from her grave and plodded along the river dressed in her white burial gown.

Night after night, the villagers saw her.

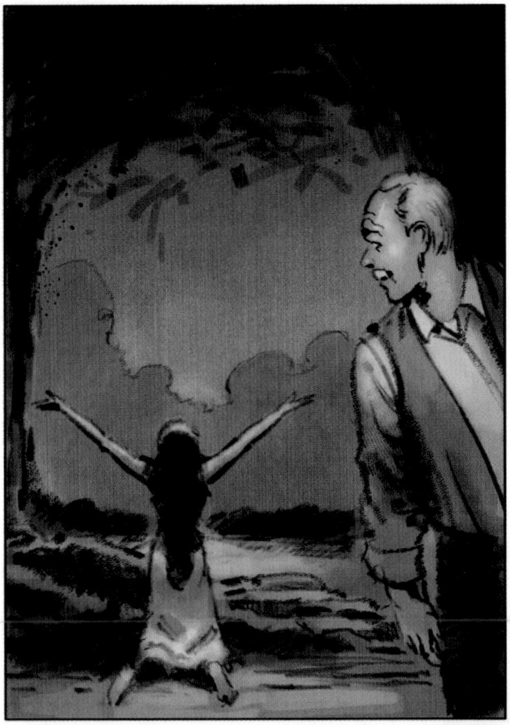

But they mostly heard her crying outside.

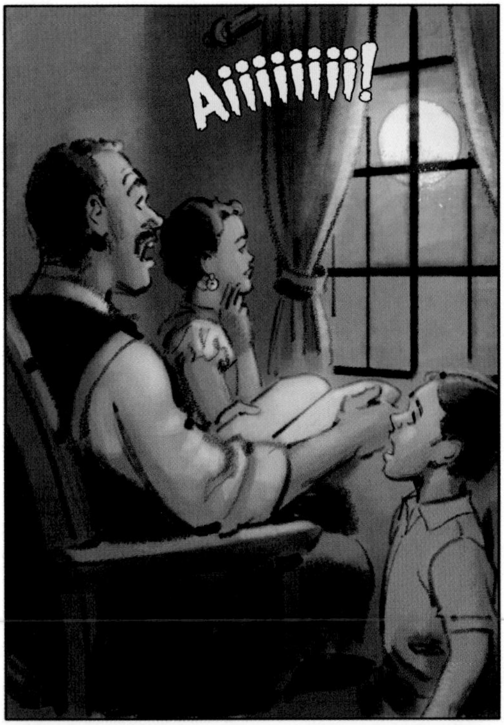
Aiiiiiiii!

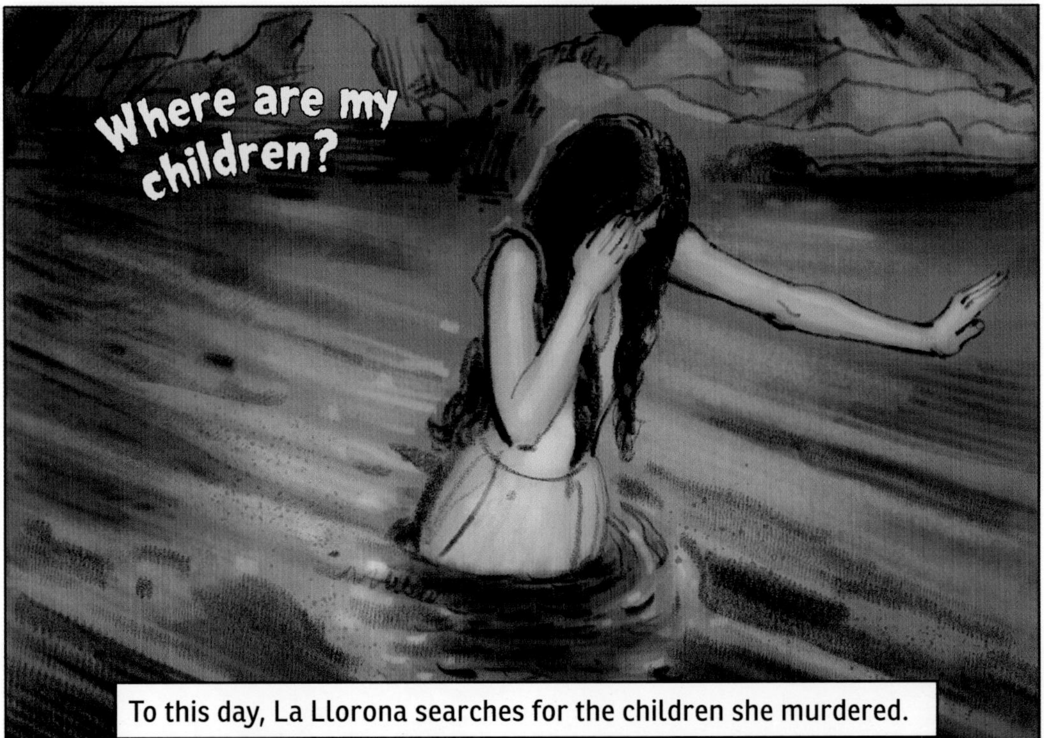
Where are my children?
To this day, La Llorona searches for the children she murdered.

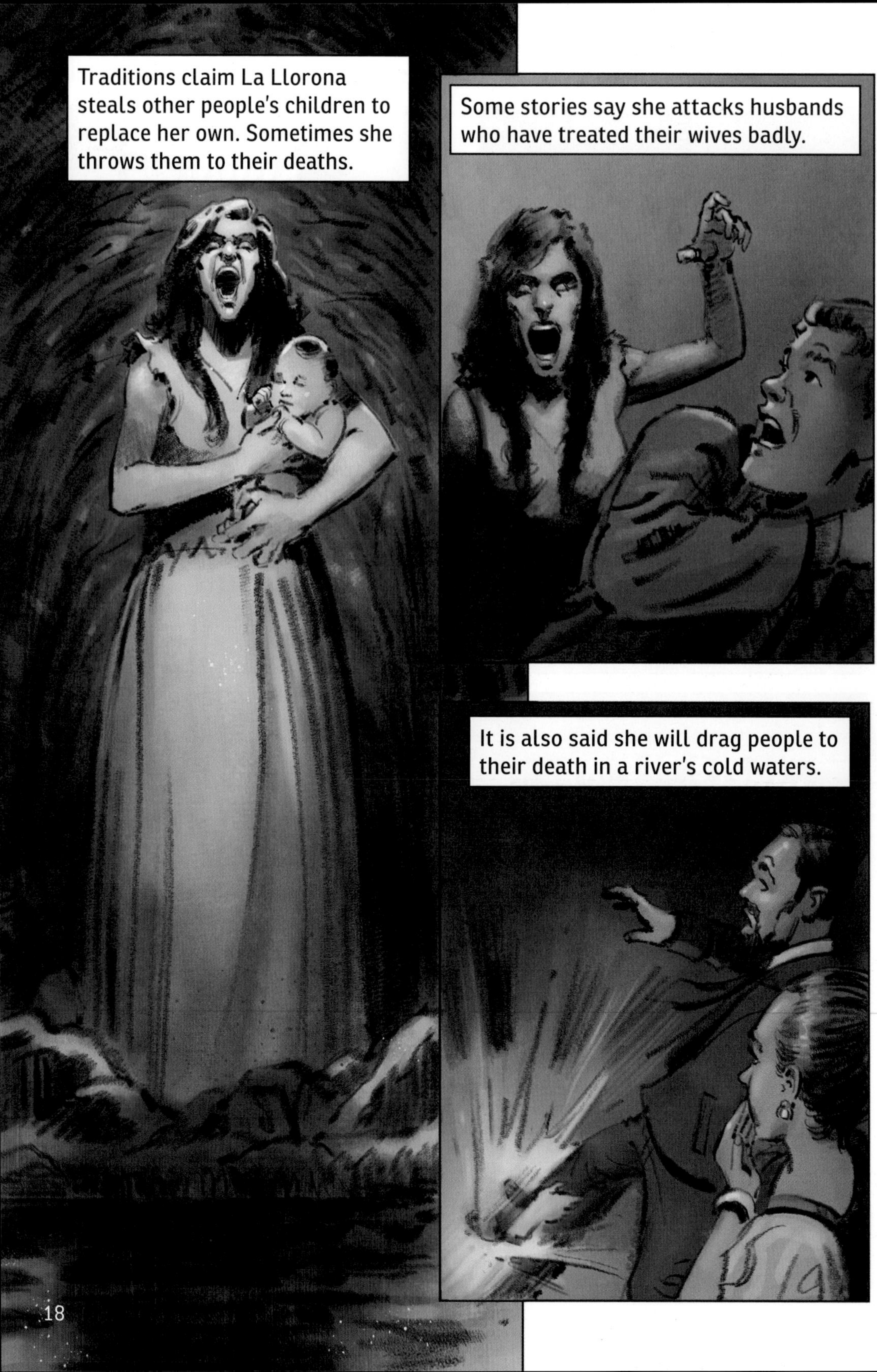
Traditions claim La Llorona steals other people's children to replace her own. Sometimes she throws them to their deaths.
Some stories say she attacks husbands who have treated their wives badly.
It is also said she will drag people to their death in a river's cold waters.

In some tales, La Llorona has the head of a wild horse.

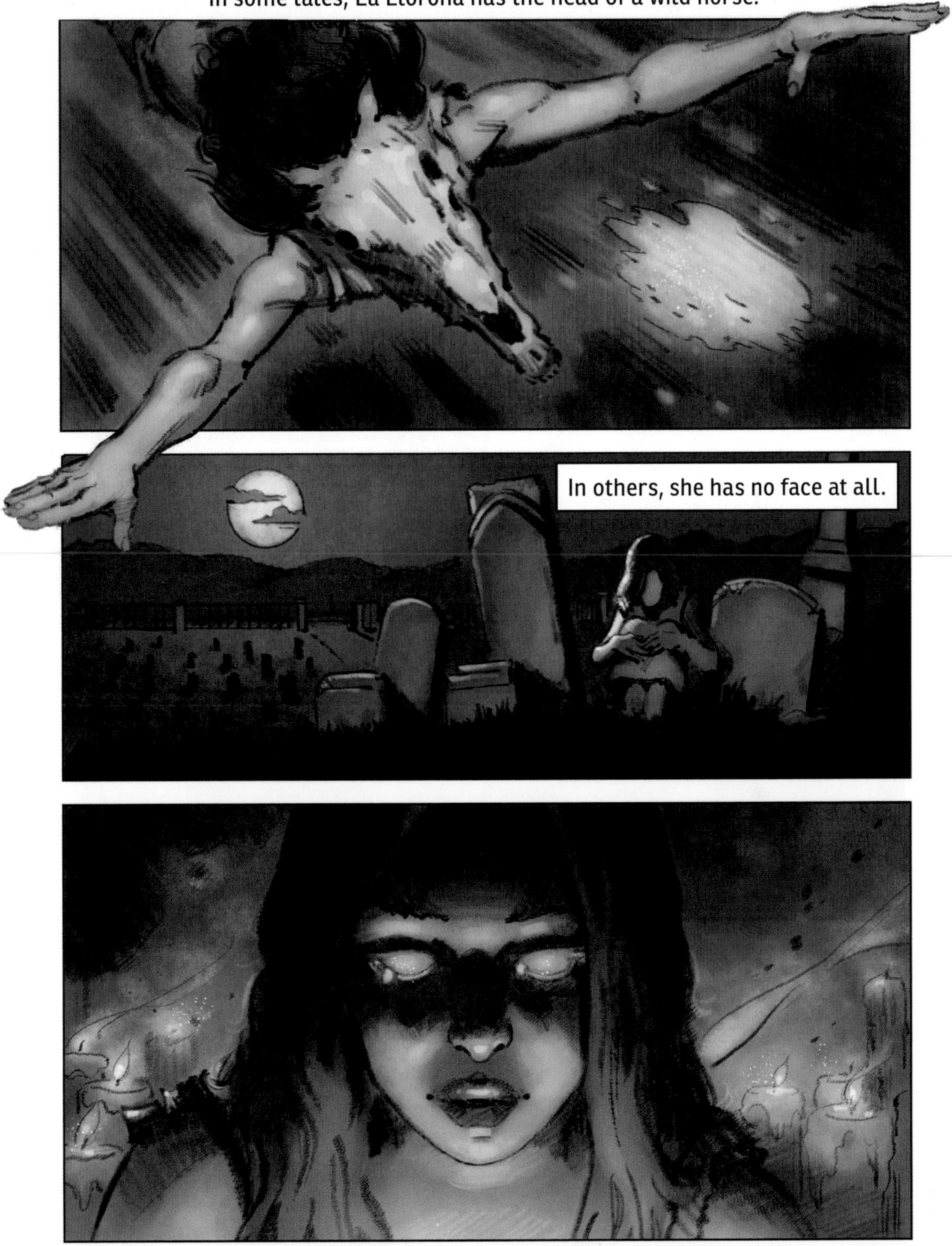
In others, she has no face at all.

But no matter what version is told, La Llorona has remained a tragic tale of jealousy, revenge, and death.

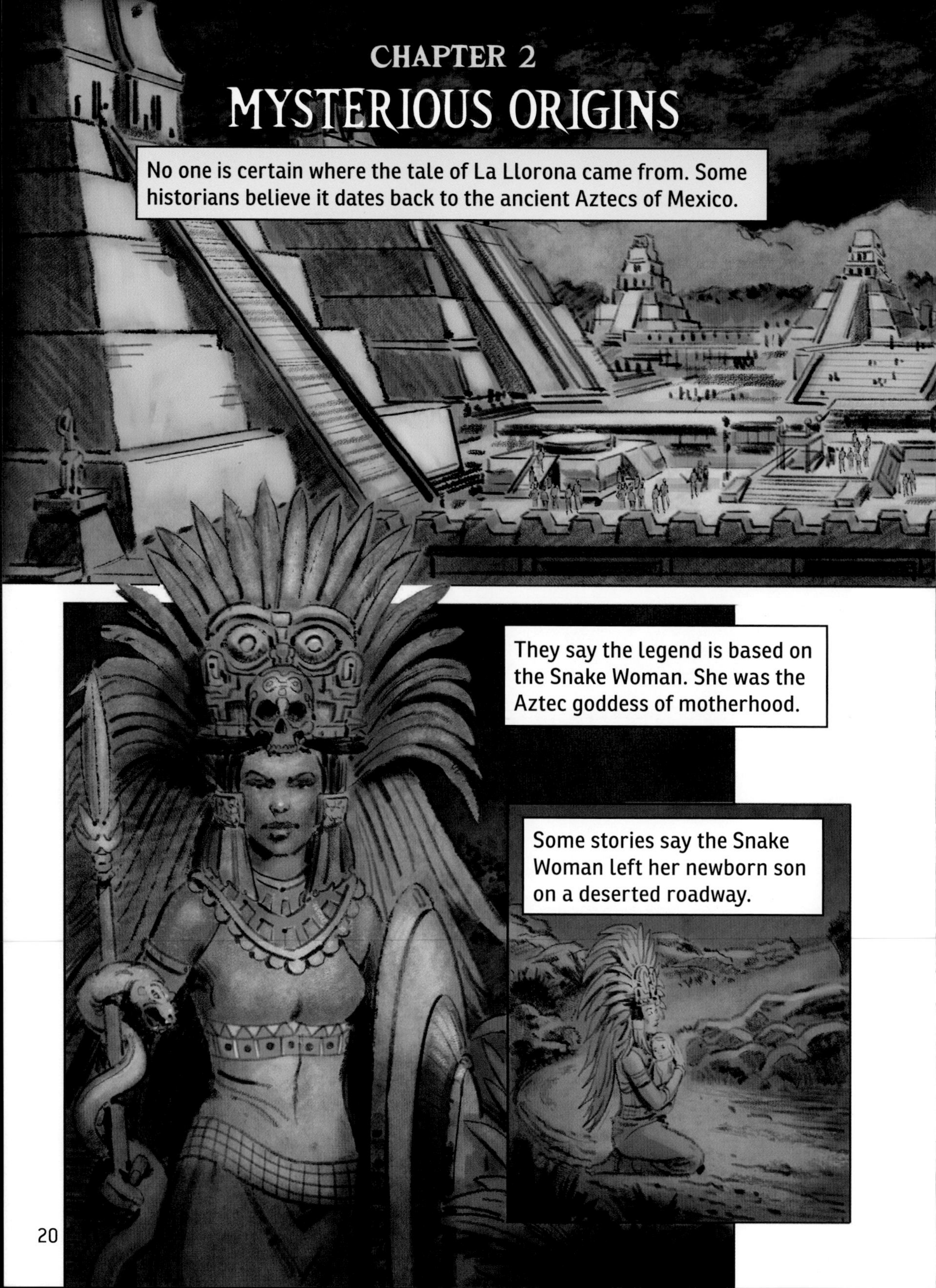
CHAPTER 2
MYSTERIOUS ORIGINS
No one is certain where the tale of La Llorona came from. Some historians believe it dates back to the ancient Aztecs of Mexico.
They say the legend is based on the Snake Woman. She was the Aztec goddess of motherhood.
Some stories say the Snake Woman left her newborn son on a deserted roadway.

Soon she was sorry for what she had done, weeping night after night.

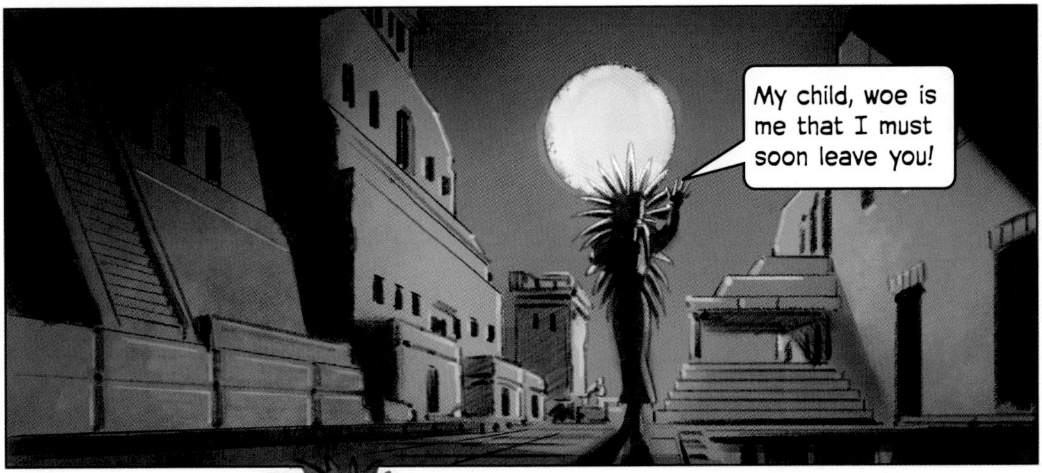
My child, woe is me that I must soon leave you!

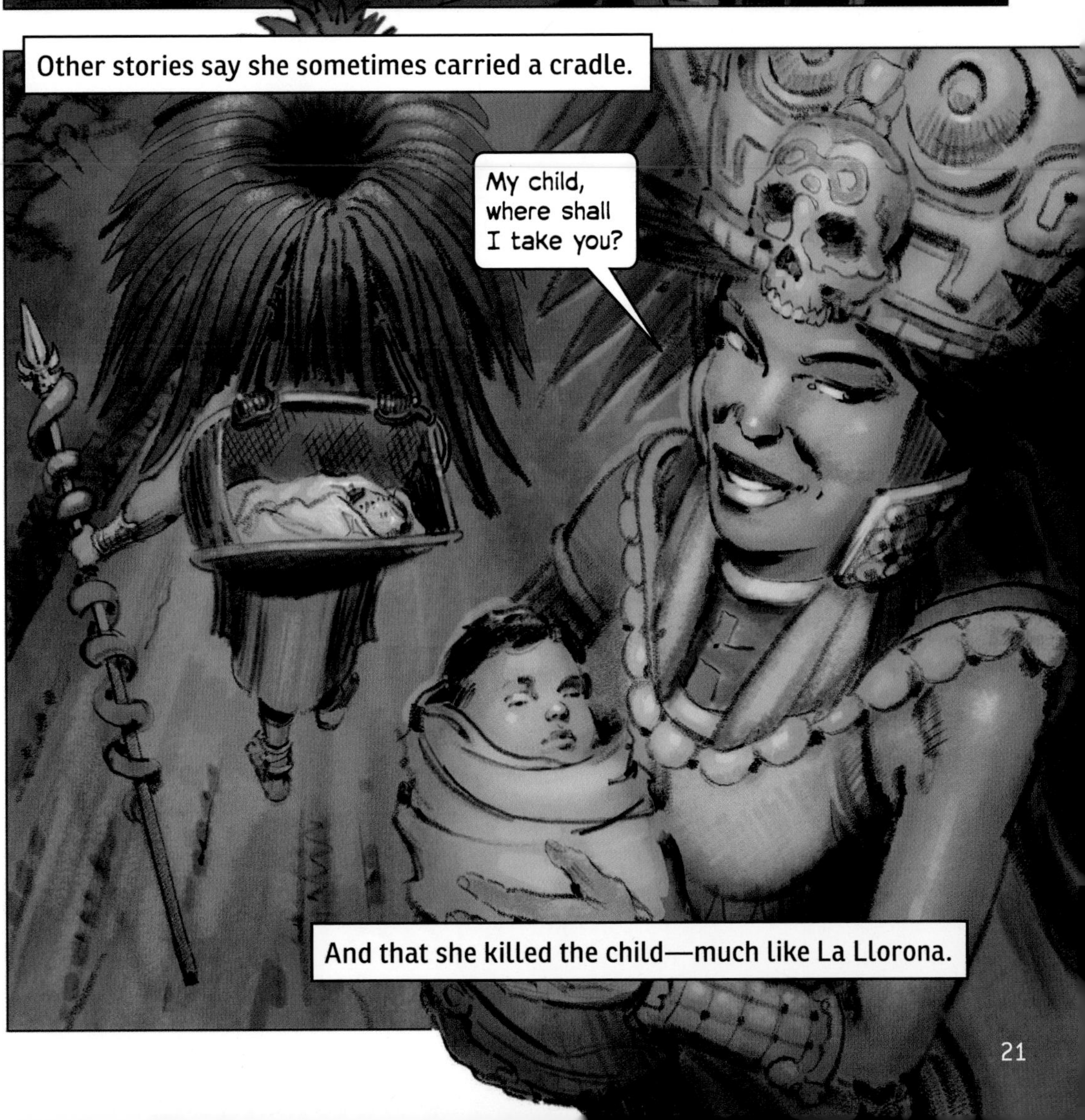
Other stories say she sometimes carried a cradle.
My child, where shall I take you?
And that she killed the child—much like La Llorona.

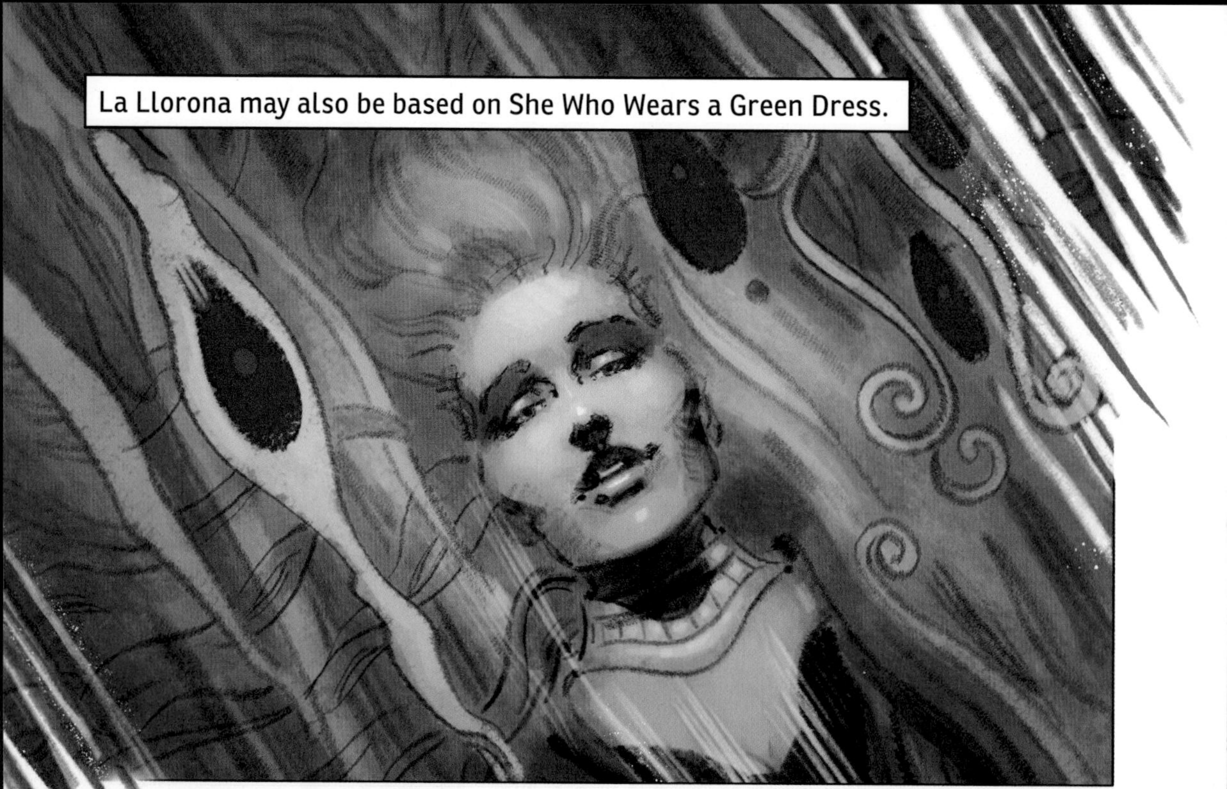
La Llorona may also be based on She Who Wears a Green Dress.

She was the Aztec goddess of Earth's waters and brought life-giving rain to feed the crops.

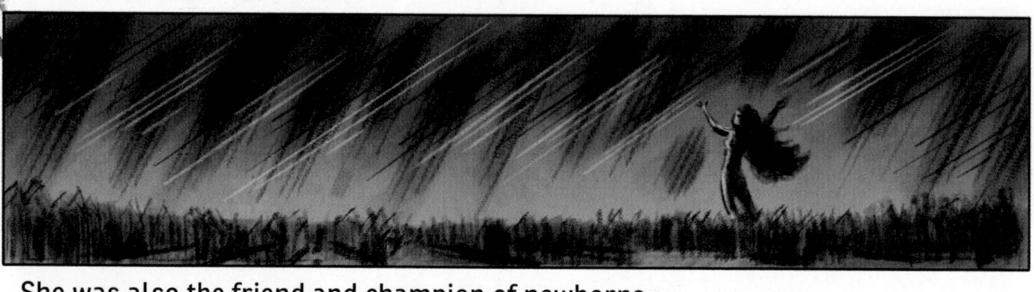

She was also the friend and champion of newborns.

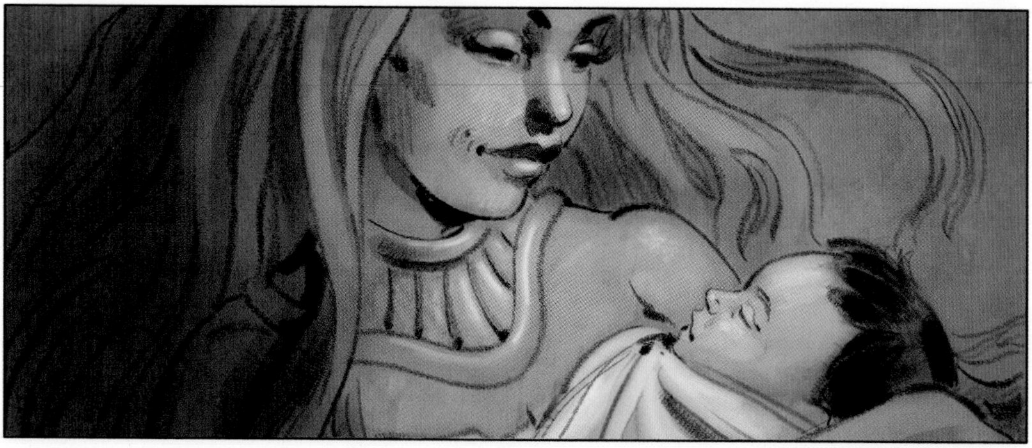

But the goddess also had a dark side. She was feared and caused terror.

She overturned boats.

And she would drown people—much like La Llorona.

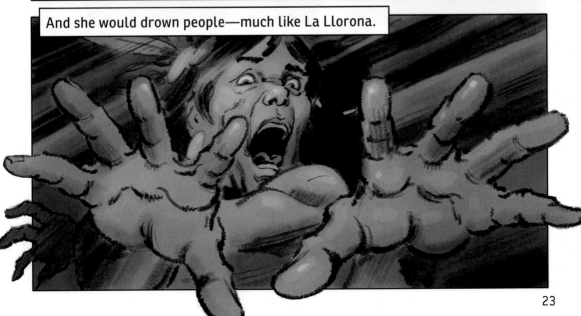

And some historians believe the story of La Llorona dates back to 16th-century Germany.

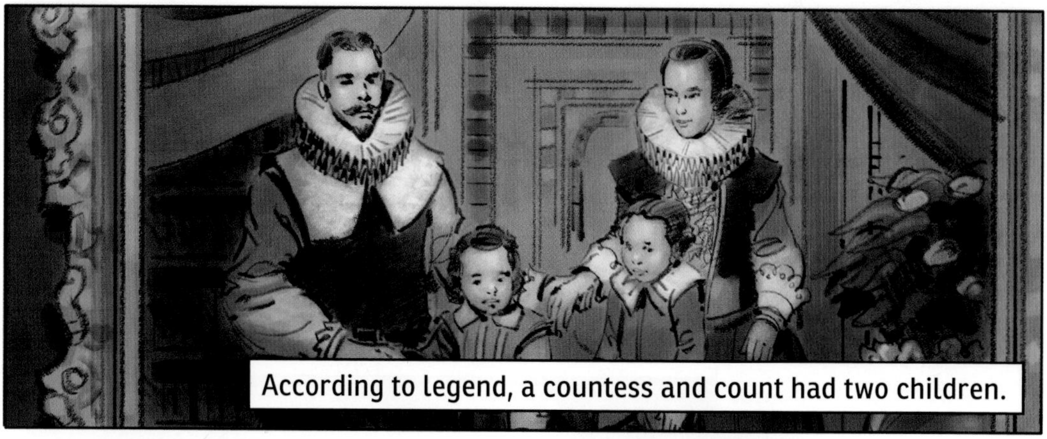
According to legend, a countess and count had two children.

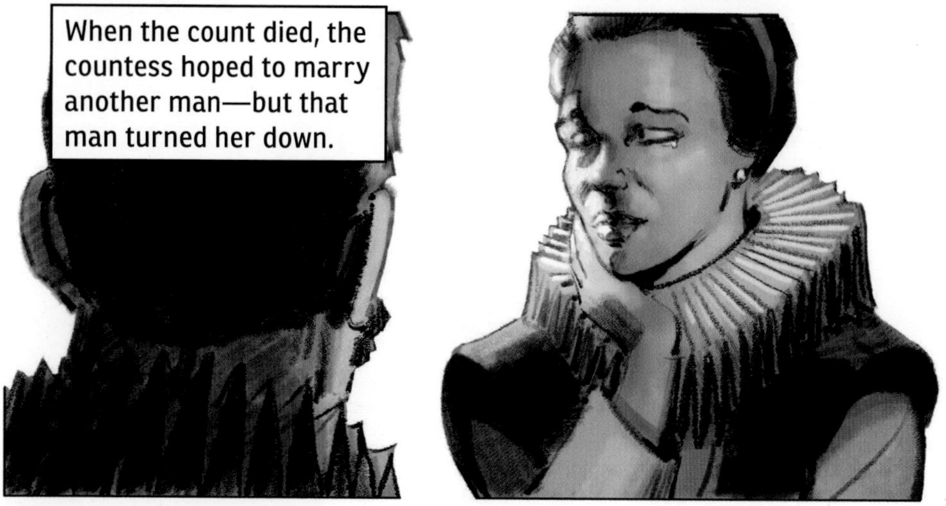
When the count died, the countess hoped to marry another man—but that man turned her down.

Believing the man did not want her children, the countess killed them.

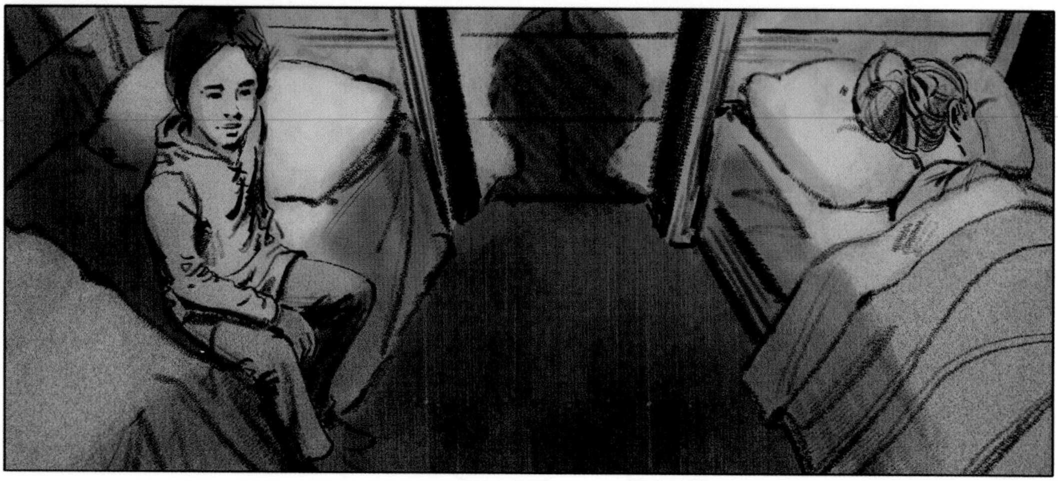

The countess hoped her act would change the man's mind, but it did not.

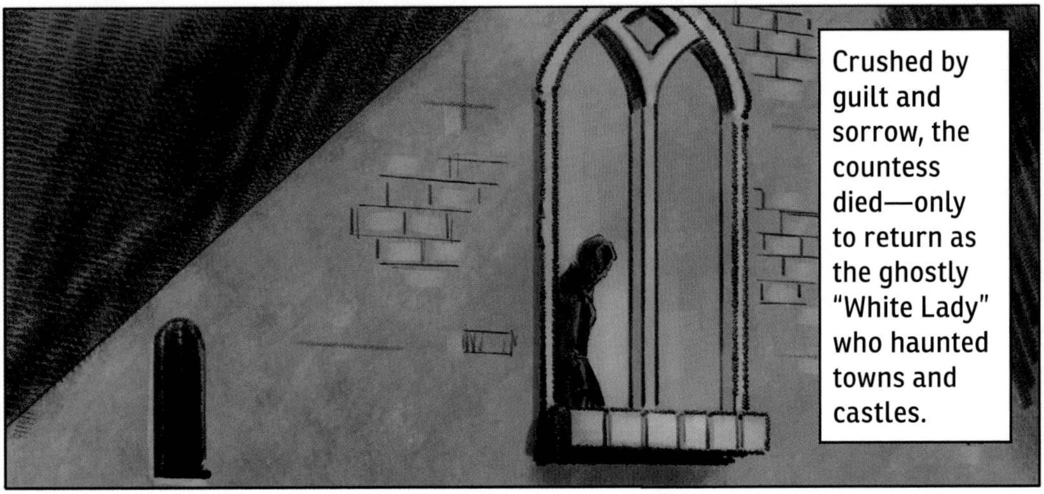
Crushed by guilt and sorrow, the countess died—only to return as the ghostly "White Lady" who haunted towns and castles.

From Aztec goddesses to Germany's White Lady, the possible origins of Latin America's Weeping Woman are frightening.

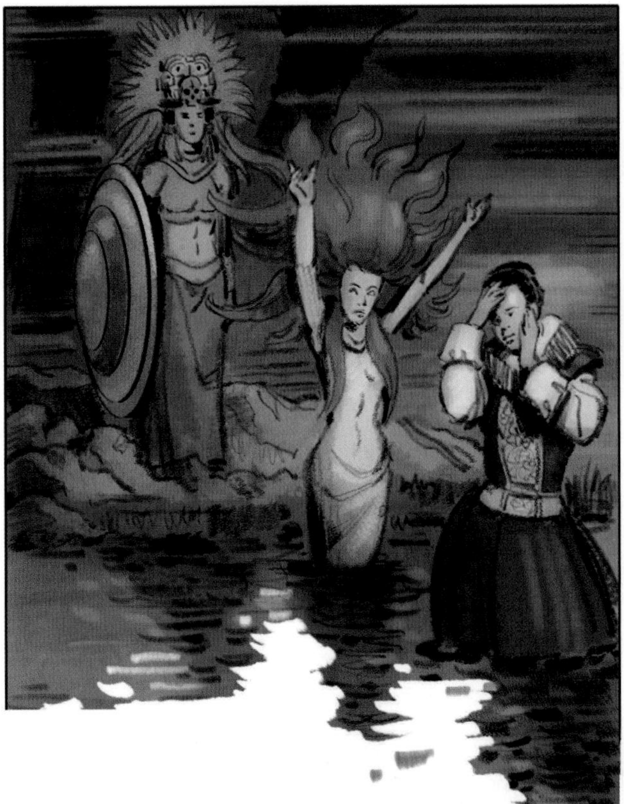

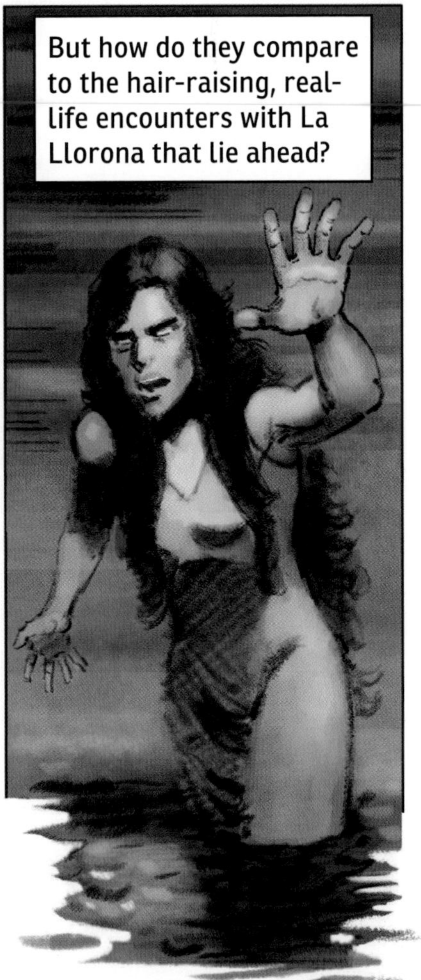
But how do they compare to the hair-raising, real-life encounters with La Llorona that lie ahead?

CHAPTER 3
THE WAILING SKULL

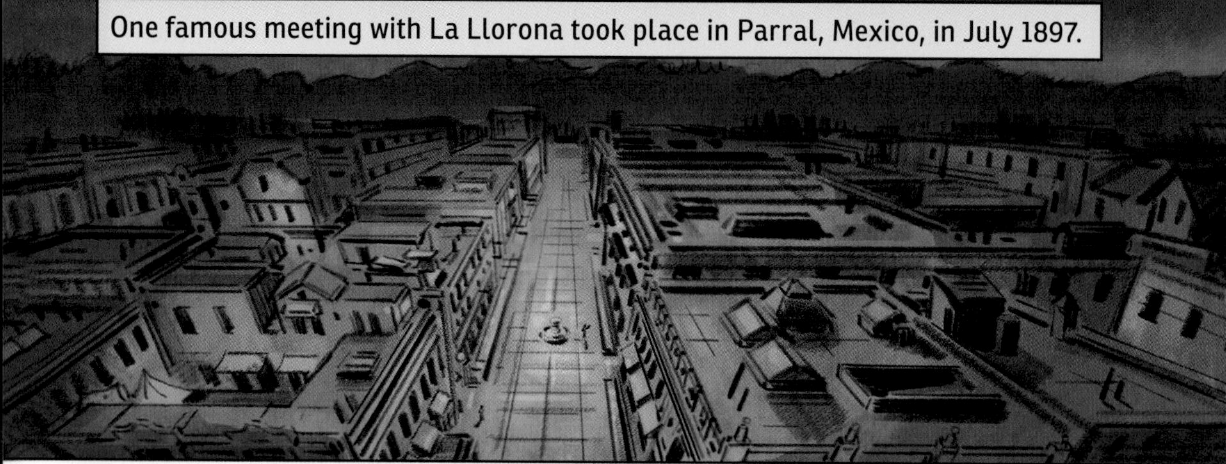
One famous meeting with La Llorona took place in Parral, Mexico, in July 1897.

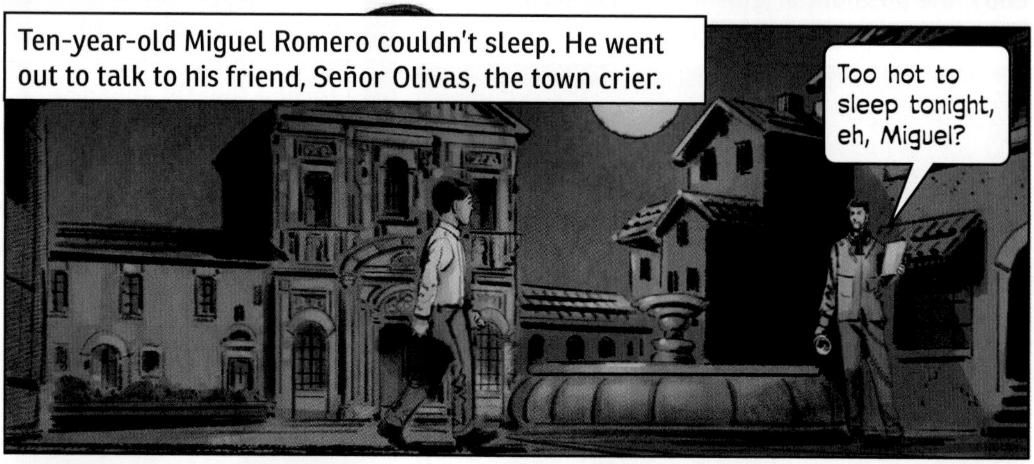
Ten-year-old Miguel Romero couldn't sleep. He went out to talk to his friend, Señor Olivas, the town crier.
Too hot to sleep tonight, eh, Miguel?

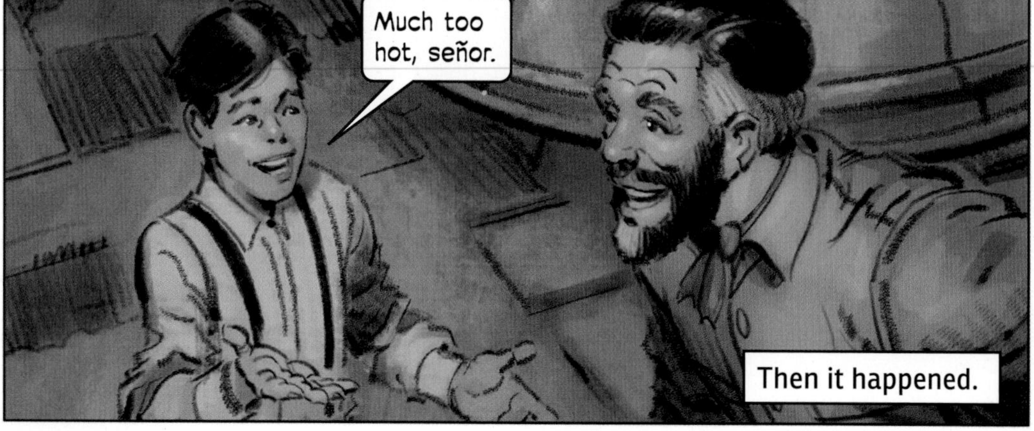
Much too hot, señor.
Then it happened.

A mysterious figure suddenly appeared. It spoke in a trembling voice.

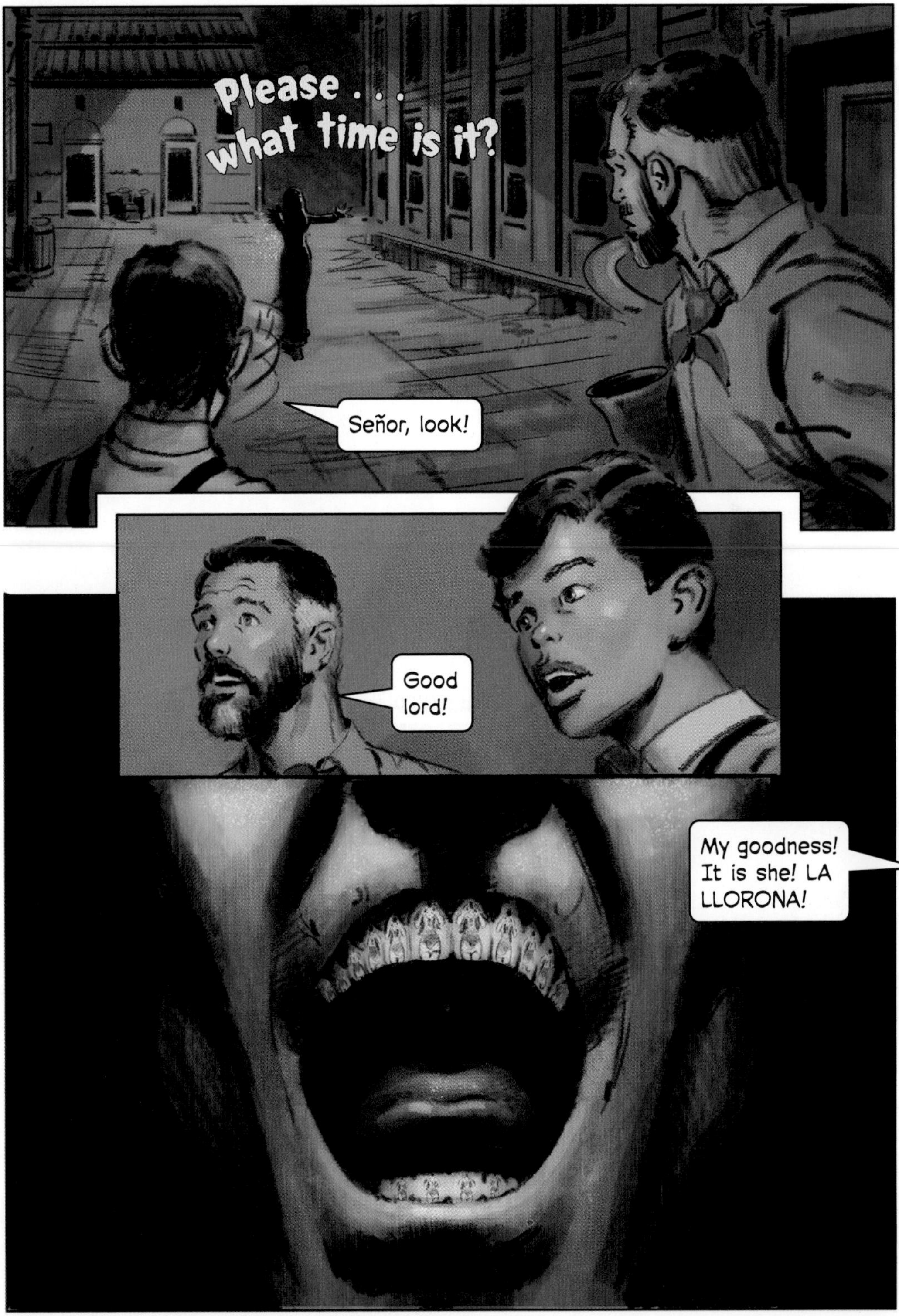
Please . . . what time is it?
Señor, look!
Good lord!
My goodness! It is she! LA LLORONA!

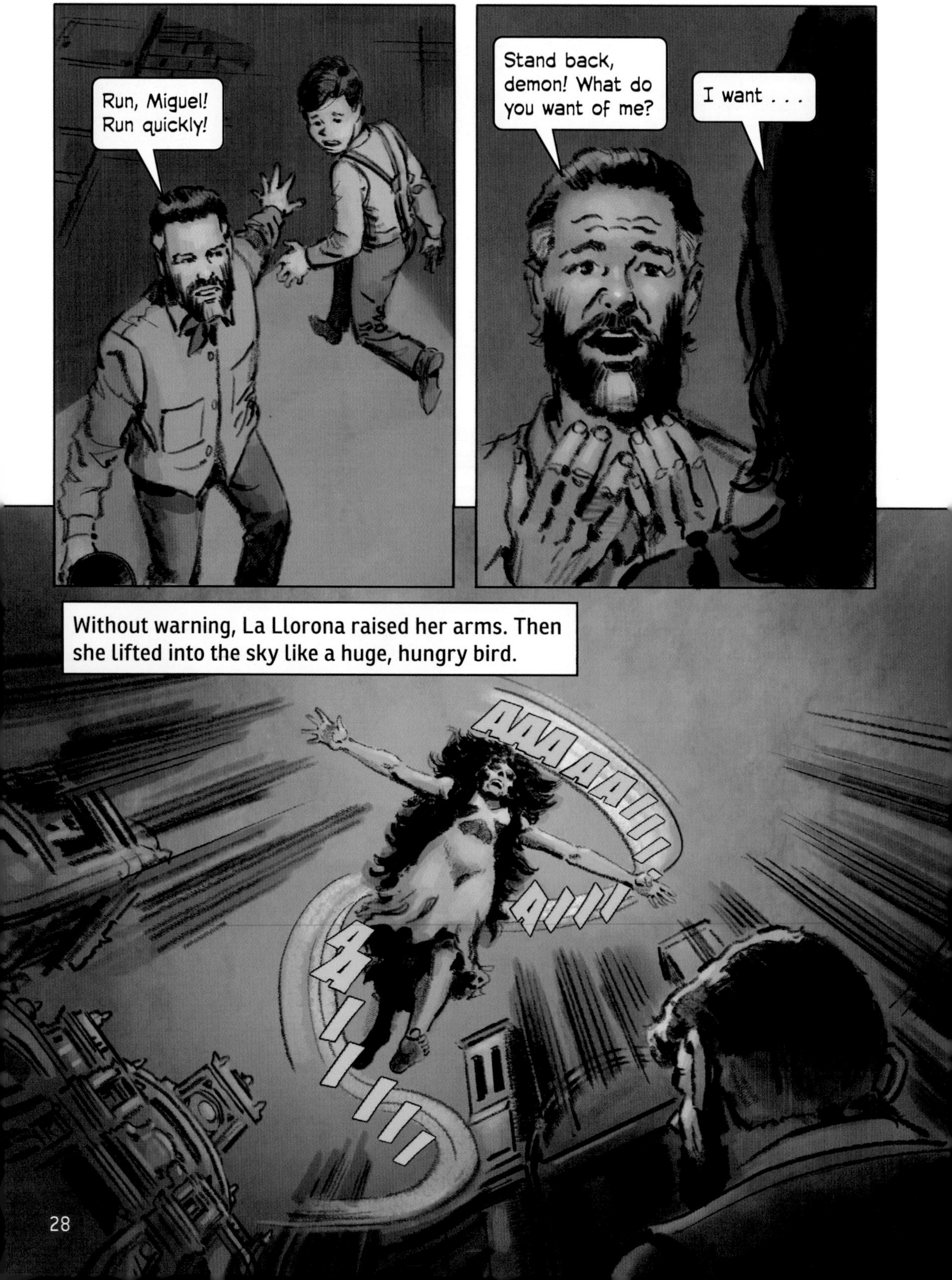
Run, Miguel! Run quickly!
Stand back, demon! What do you want of me?
I want . . .
Without warning, La Llorona raised her arms. Then she lifted into the sky like a huge, hungry bird.

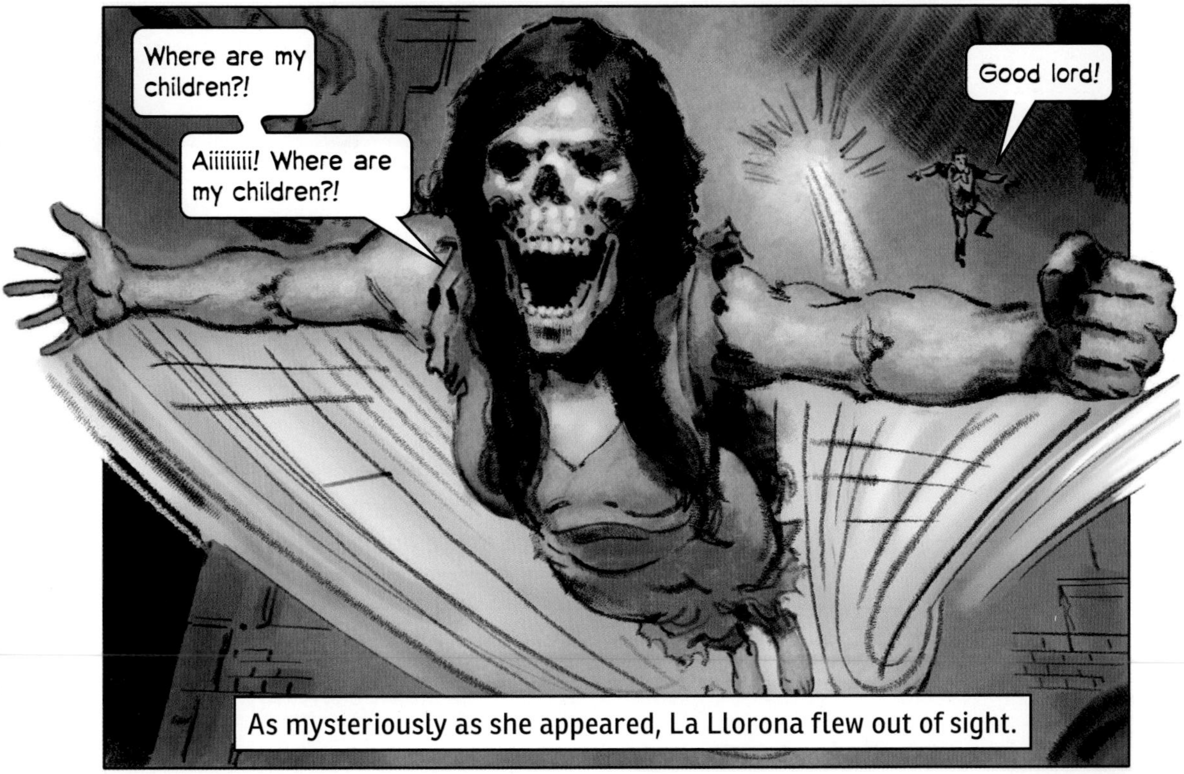
Where are my children?!
Aiiiiiiii! Where are my children?!
Good lord!
As mysteriously as she appeared, La Llorona flew out of sight.

Señor Olivas never told a single soul about his ghastly experience.

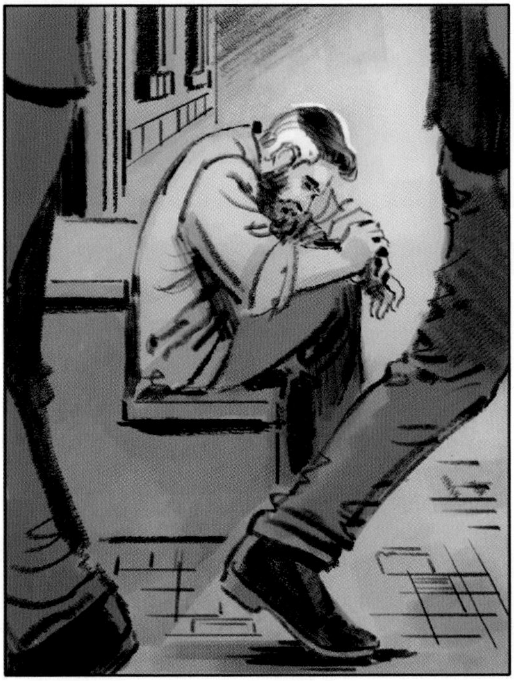

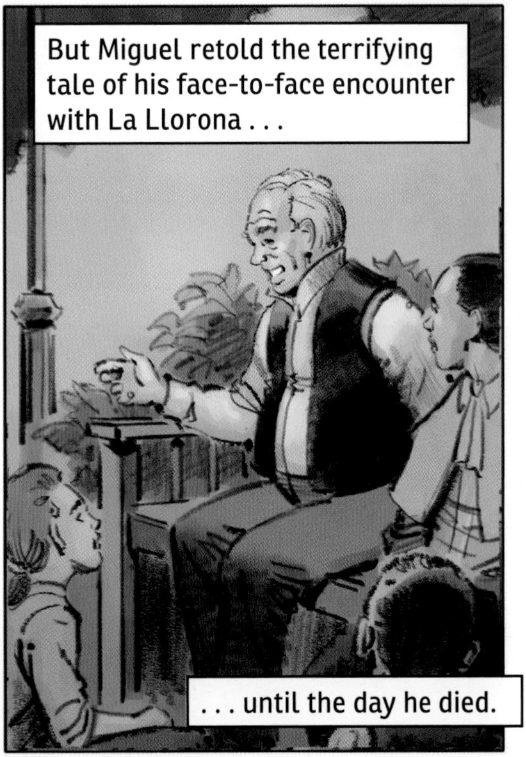
But Miguel retold the terrifying tale of his face-to-face encounter with La Llorona . . .
. . . until the day he died.

CHAPTER 4

A SIGHTING AT THE CEMETERY

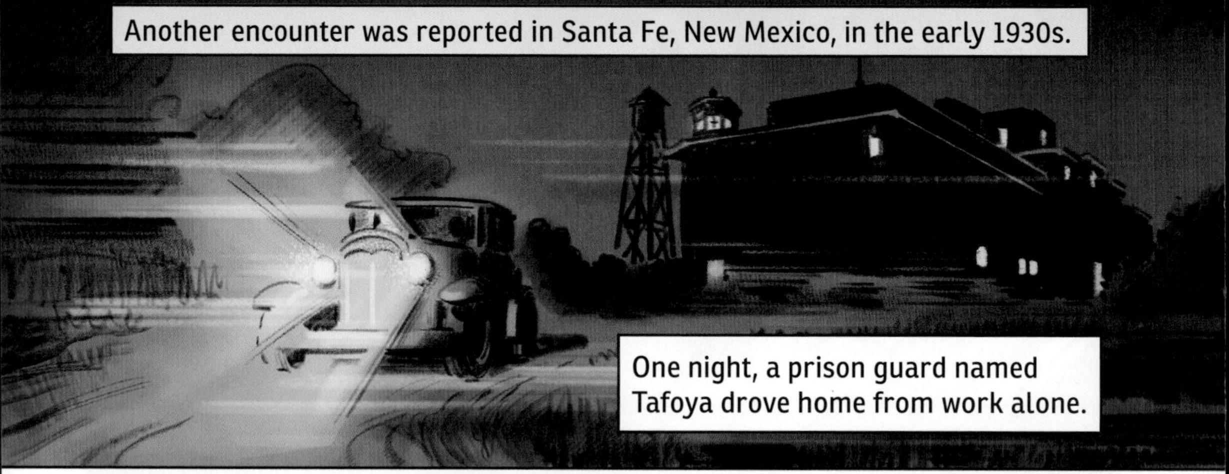
Another encounter was reported in Santa Fe, New Mexico, in the early 1930s.
One night, a prison guard named Tafoya drove home from work alone.

Suddenly . . .

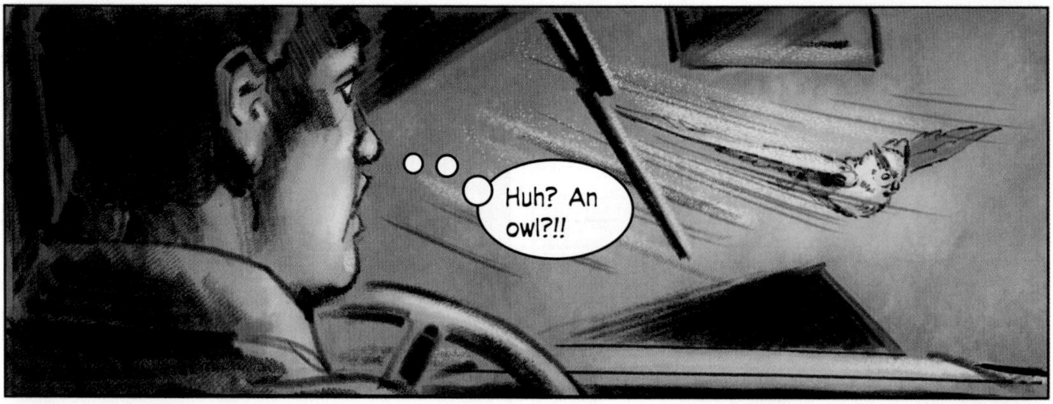
Huh? An owl?!!

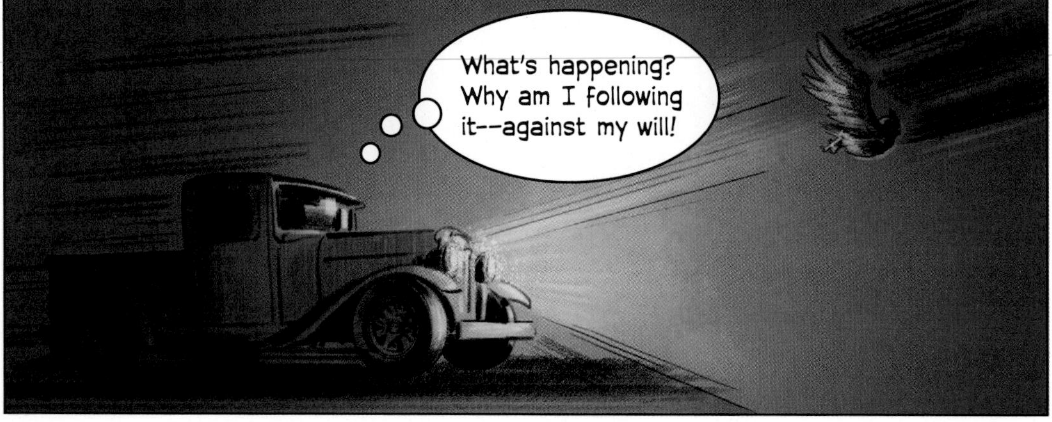
What's happening? Why am I following it--against my will!

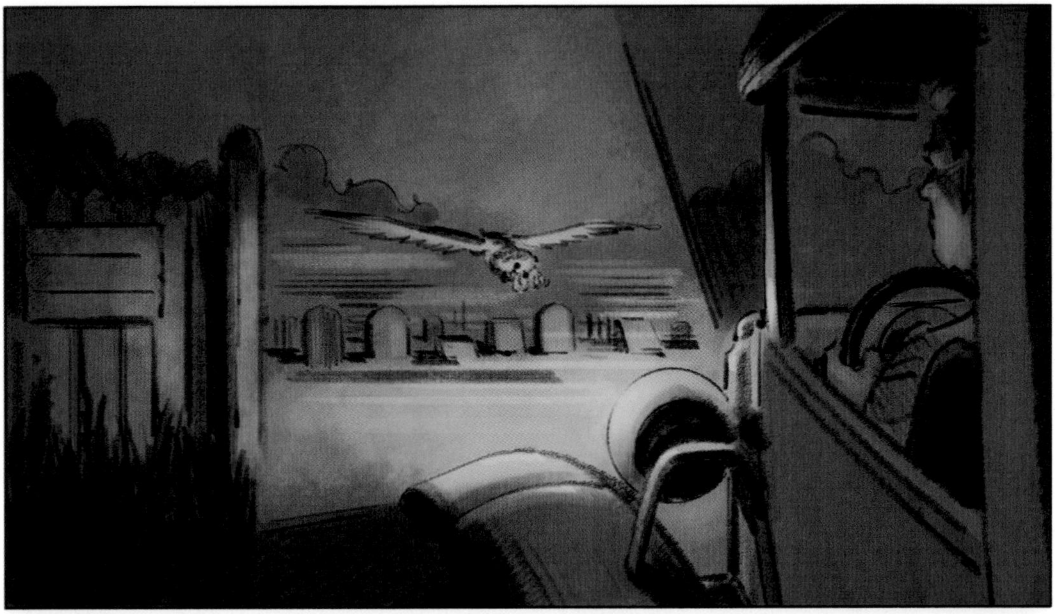

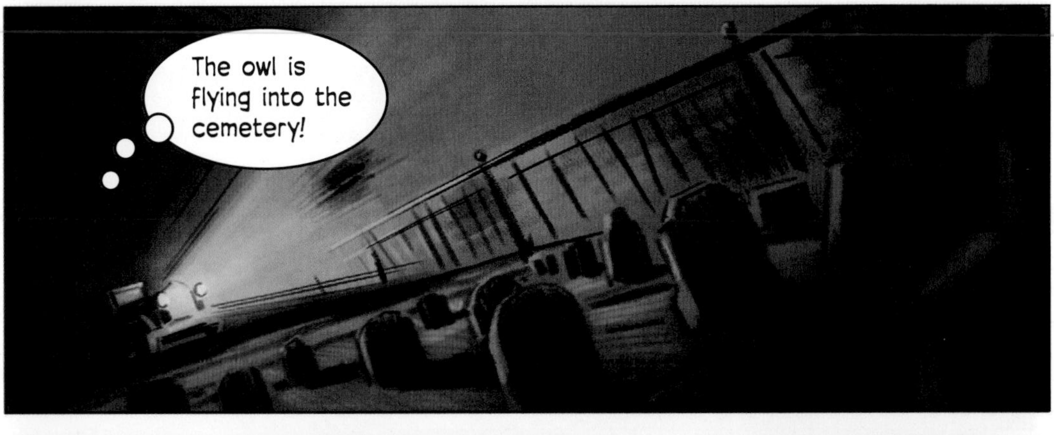
The owl is flying into the cemetery!

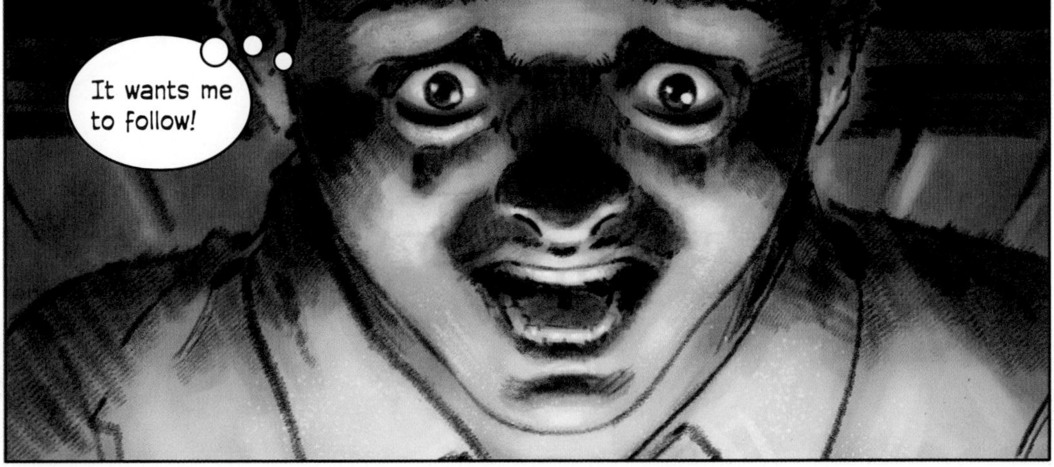
It wants me to follow!

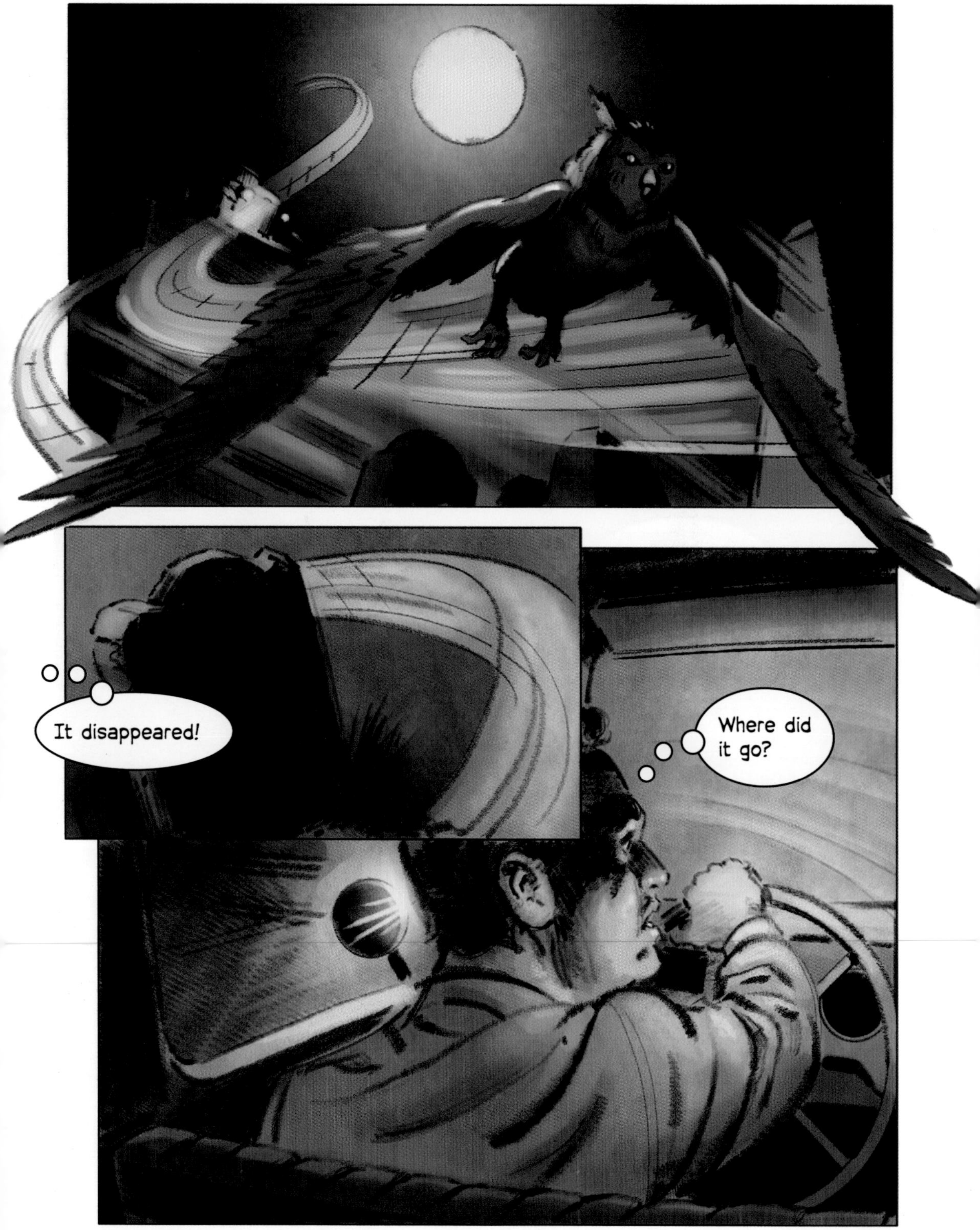
It disappeared!
Where did it go?

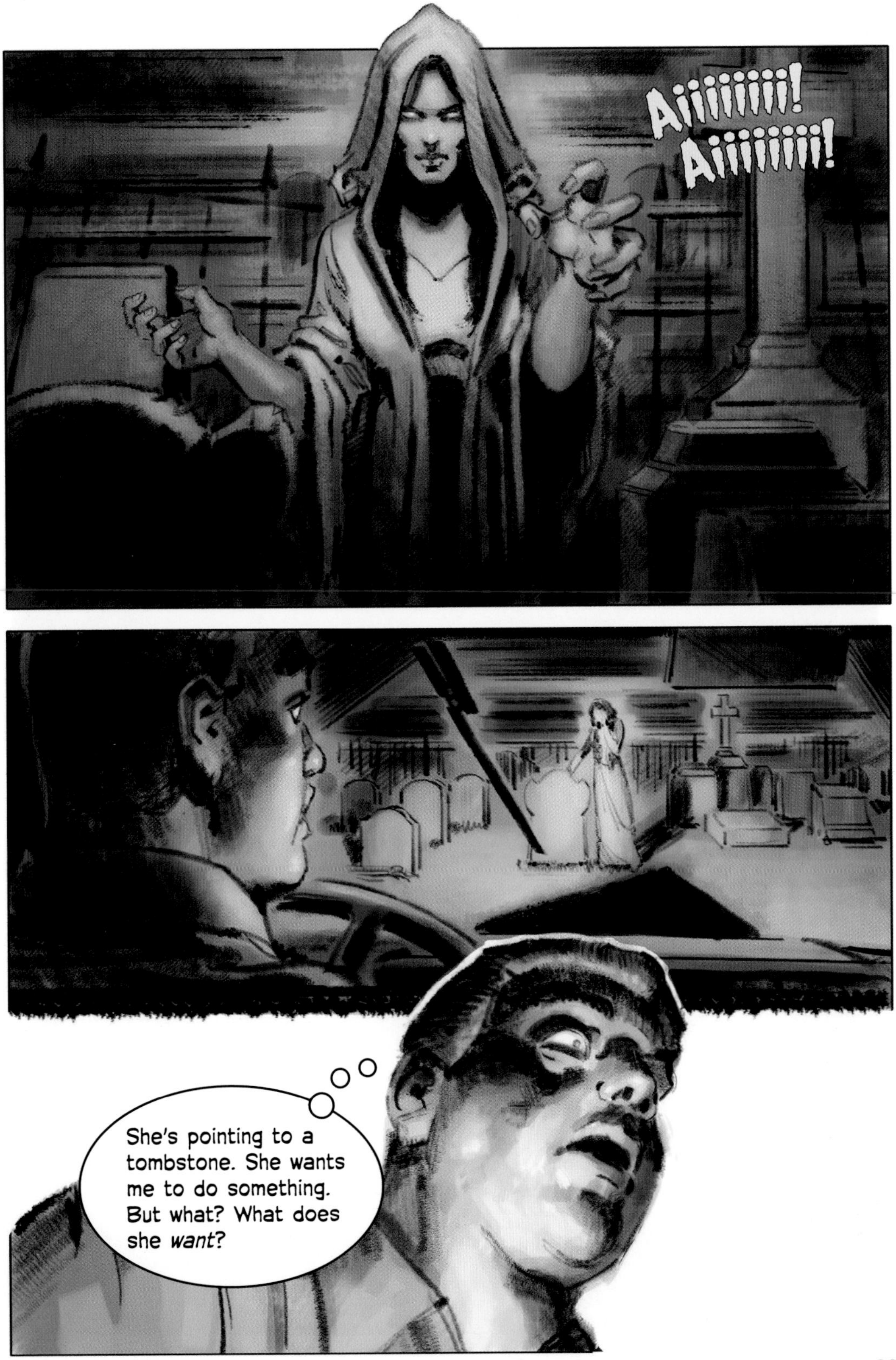
Aiiiiiiii! Aiiiiiiii!
She's pointing to a tombstone. She wants me to do something. But what? What does she *want*?

Terrified, Tafoya slammed the car into reverse and sped home.

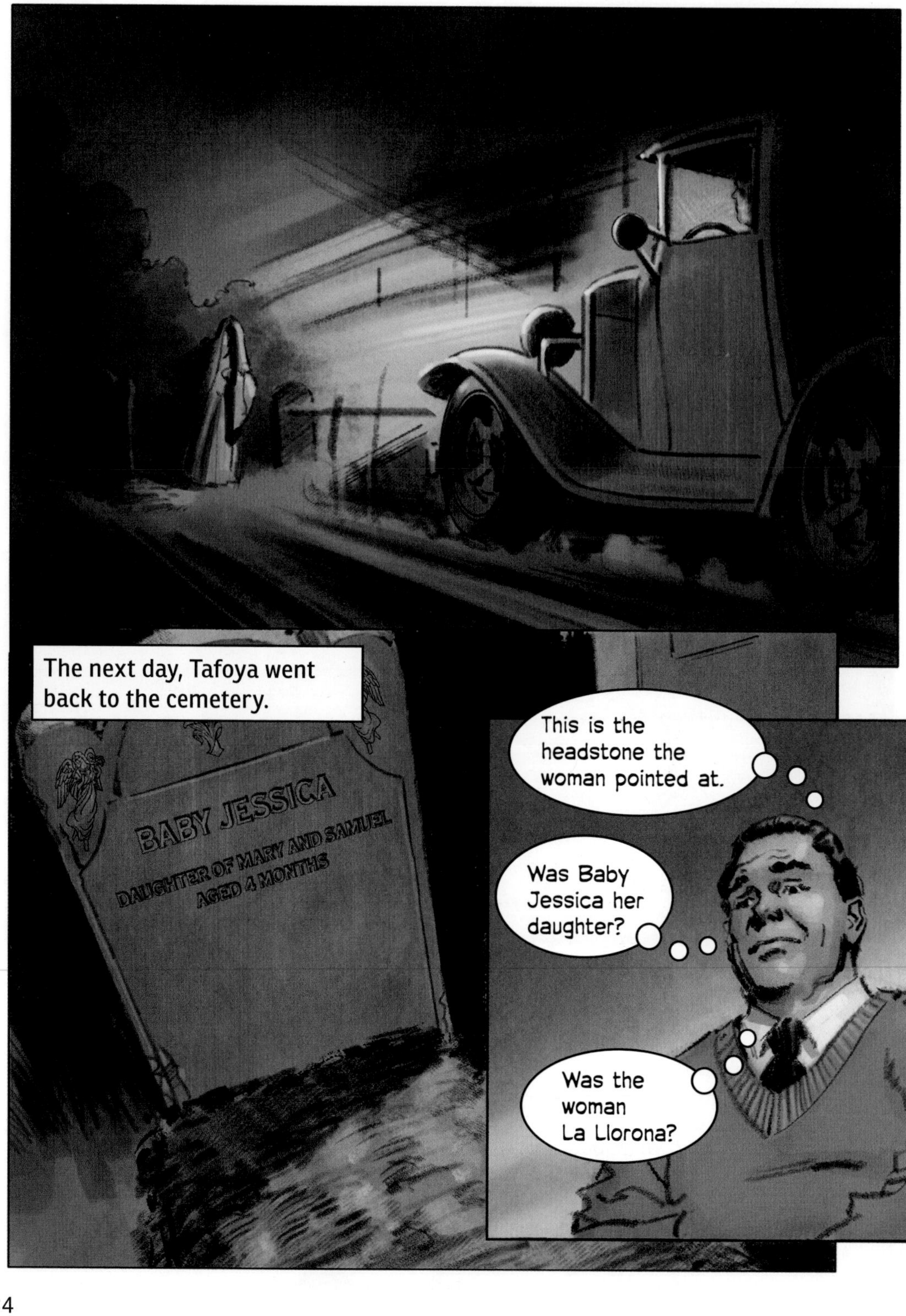
The next day, Tafoya went back to the cemetery.
BABY JESSICA
DAUGHTER OF MARY AND SAMUEL
AGED 4 MONTHS
This is the headstone the woman pointed at.
Was Baby Jessica her daughter?
Was the woman La Llorona?

No one believed Tafoya's story.

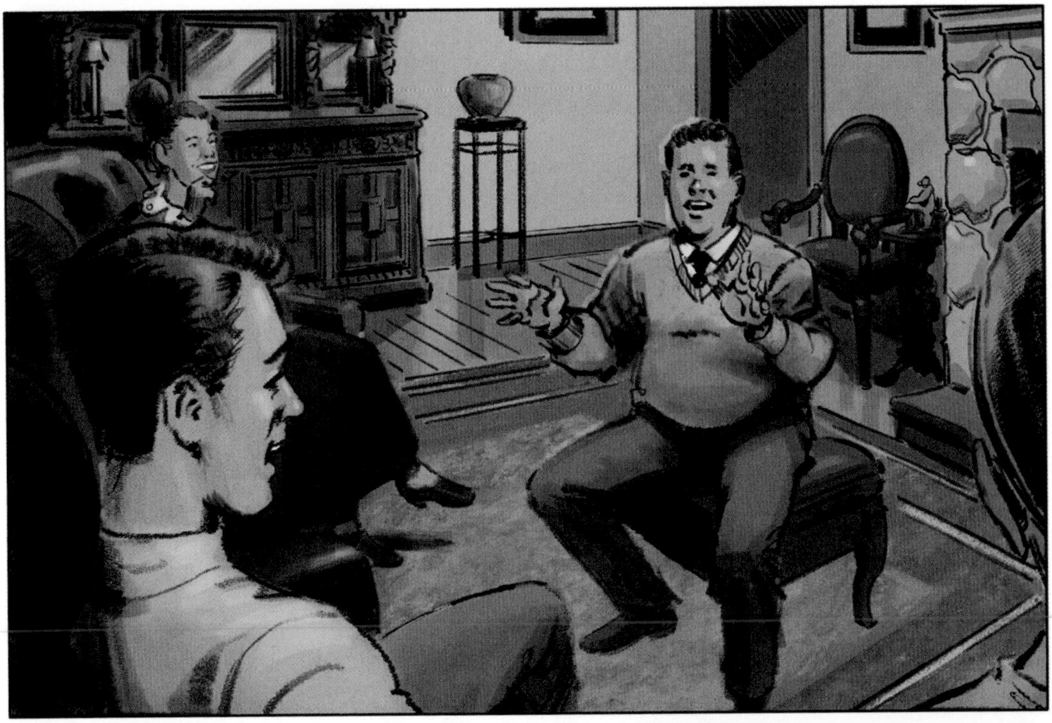

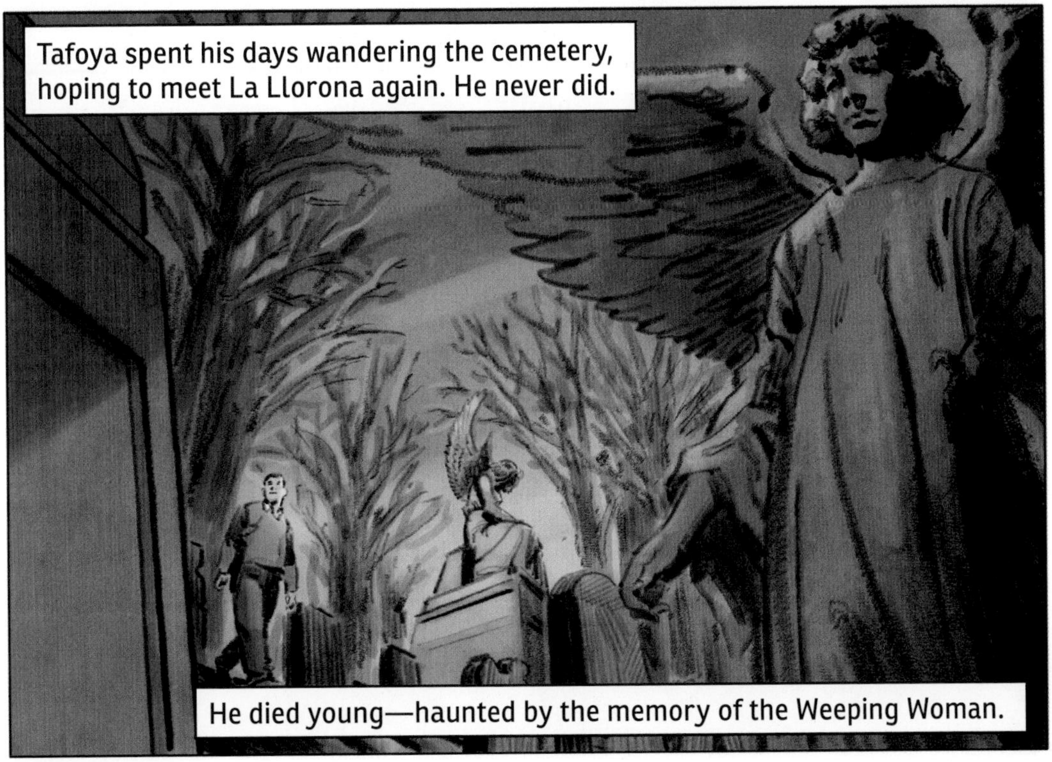
Tafoya spent his days wandering the cemetery, hoping to meet La Llorona again. He never did.
He died young—haunted by the memory of the Weeping Woman.

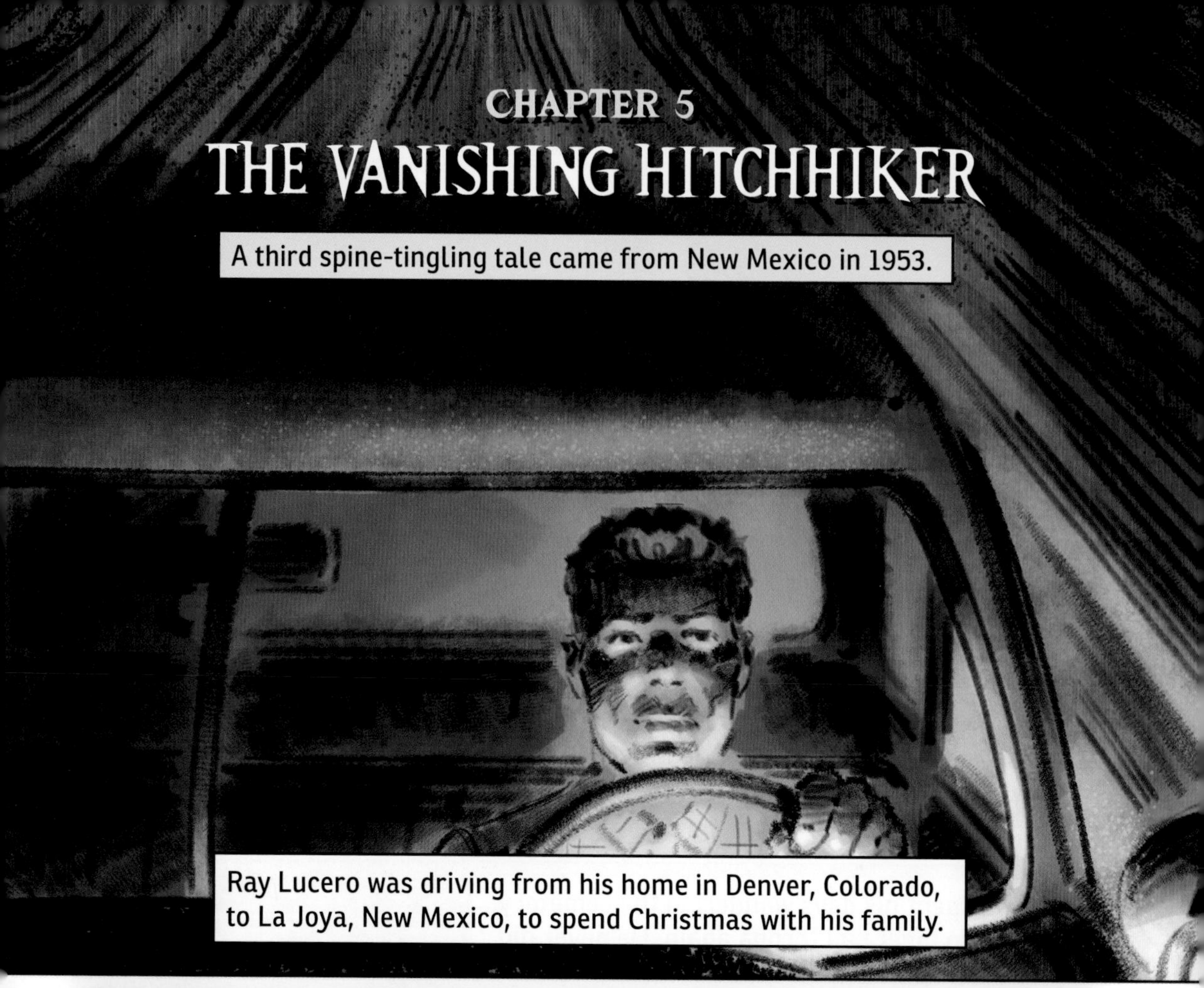
CHAPTER 5
THE VANISHING HITCHHIKER
A third spine-tingling tale came from New Mexico in 1953.
Ray Lucero was driving from his home in Denver, Colorado, to La Joya, New Mexico, to spend Christmas with his family.

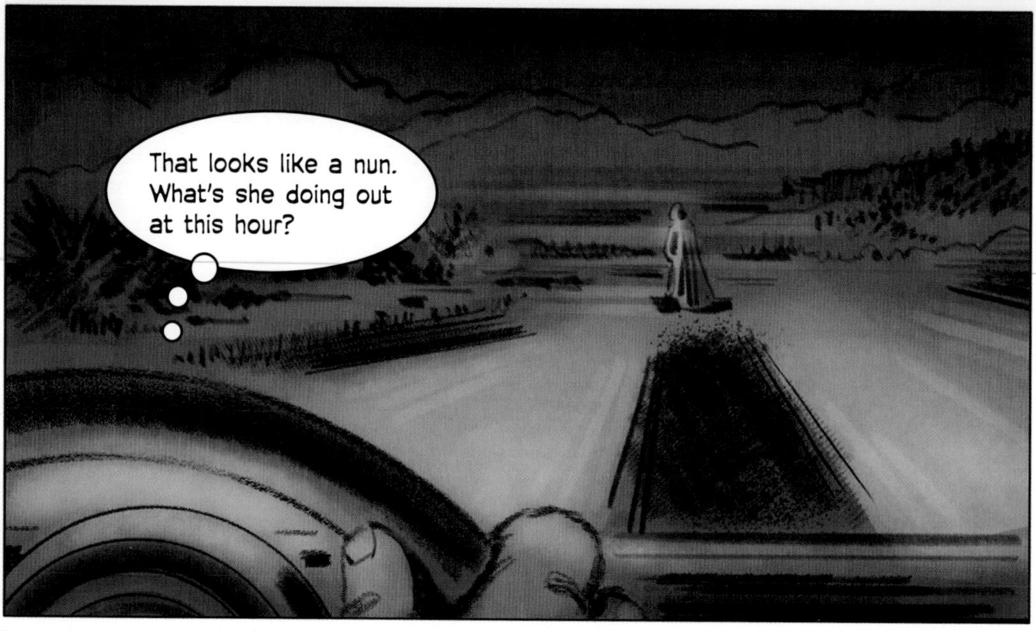
That looks like a nun. What's she doing out at this hour?

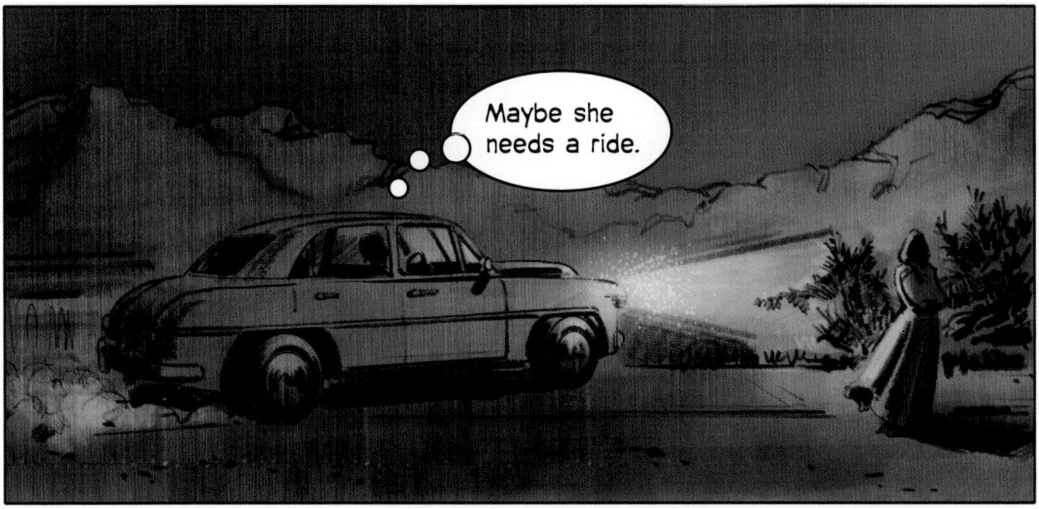
Maybe she needs a ride.

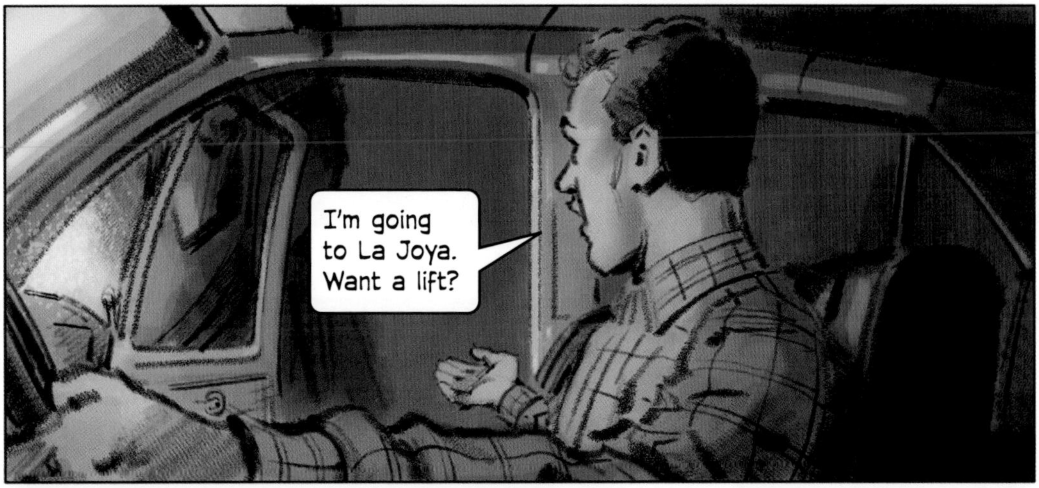
I'm going to La Joya. Want a lift?

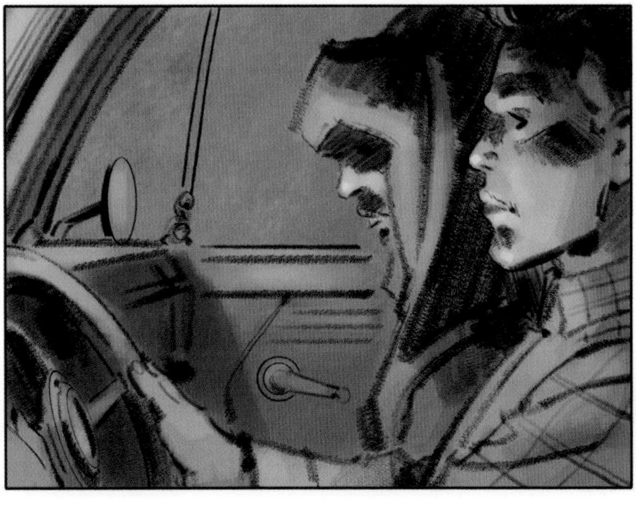

Ray and the stranger drove off into the night.

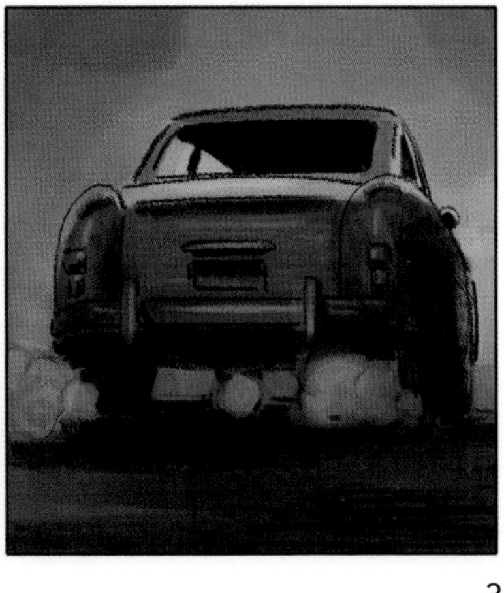

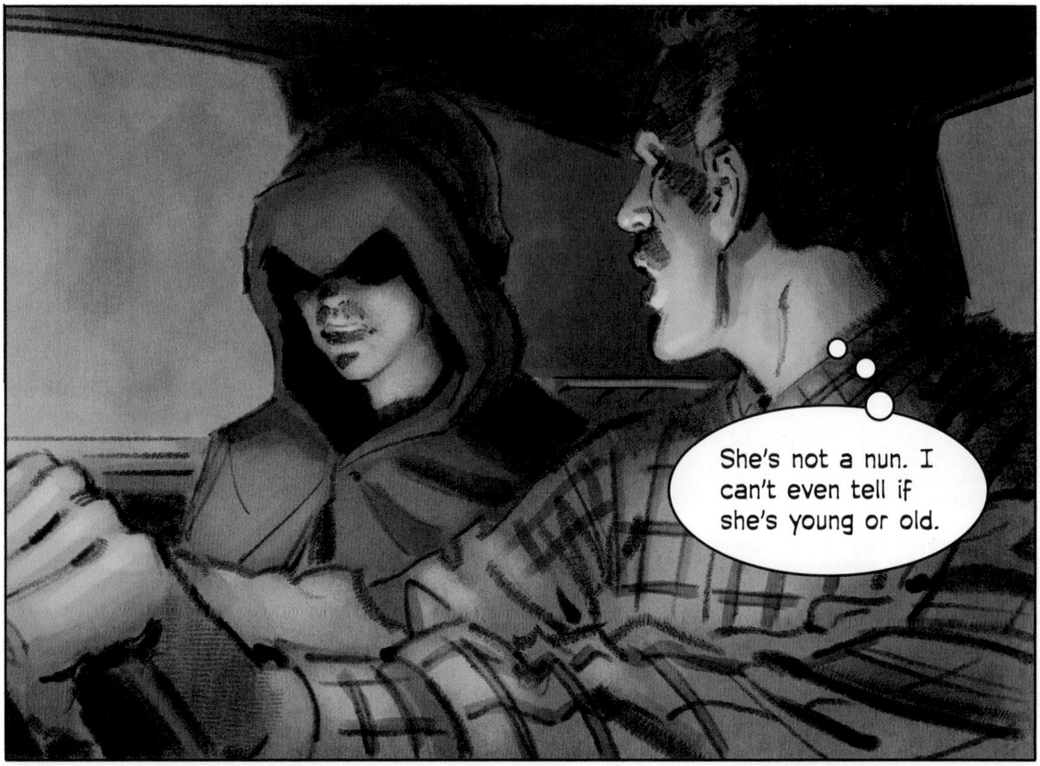
She's not a nun. I can't even tell if she's young or old.

Ray tried talking to his passenger.

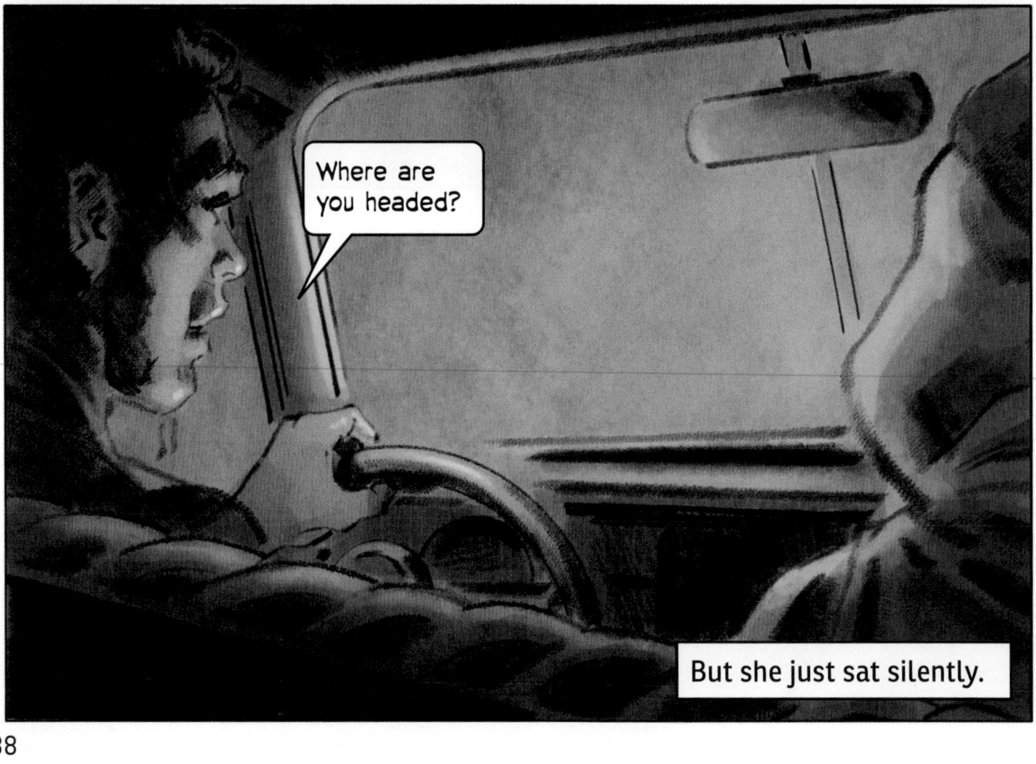
Where are you headed?
But she just sat silently.

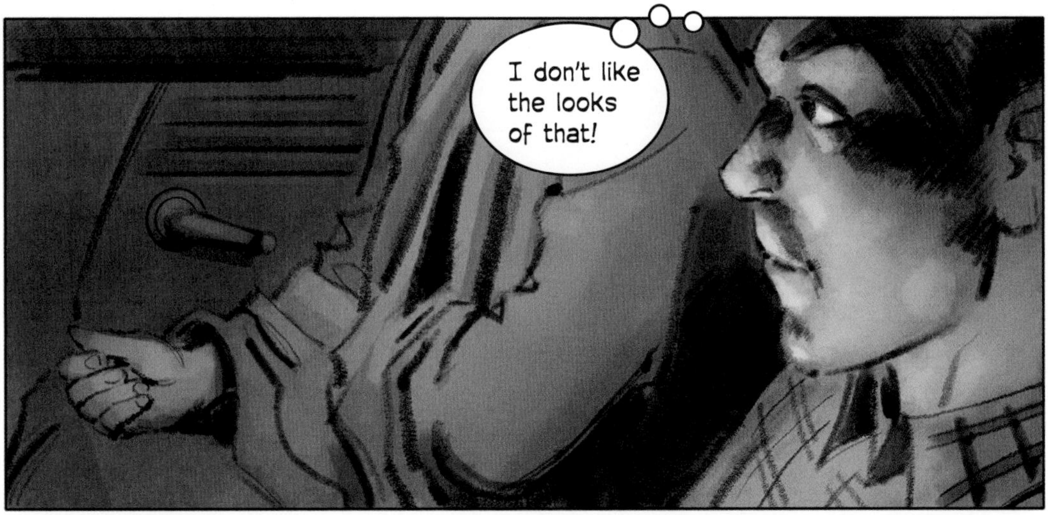
I don't like the looks of that!

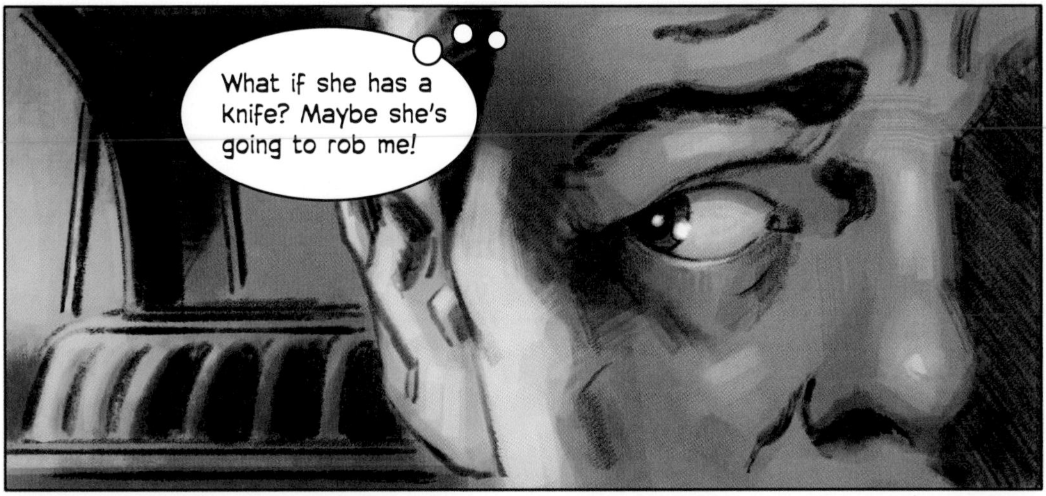
What if she has a knife? Maybe she's going to rob me!

Suddenly Ray smelled sulfur.

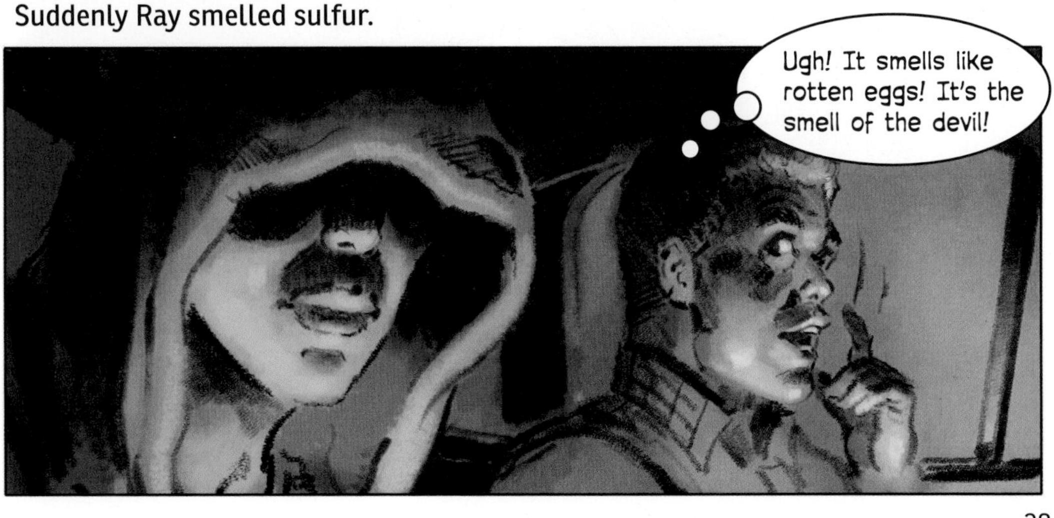
Ugh! It smells like rotten eggs! It's the smell of the devil!

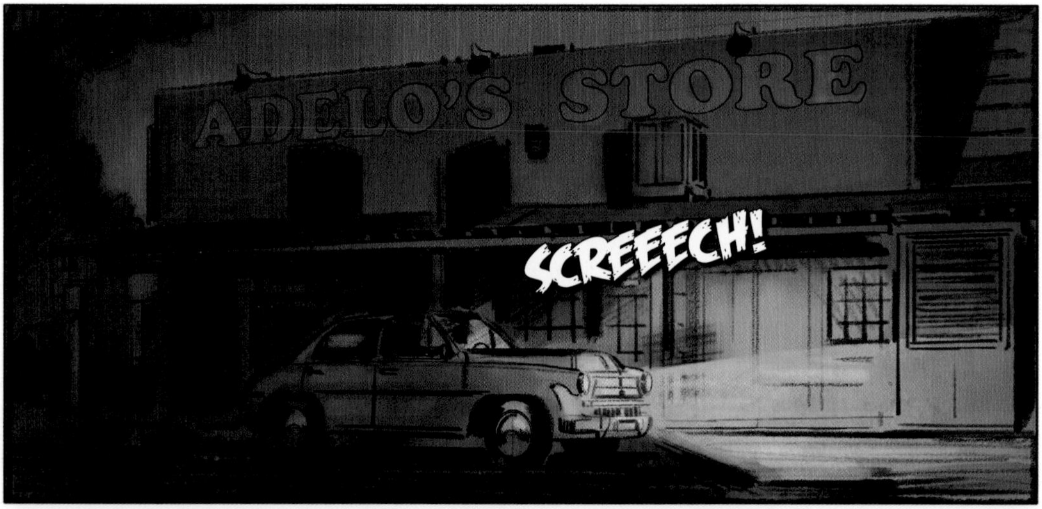
ADELO'S STORE
SCREEECH!

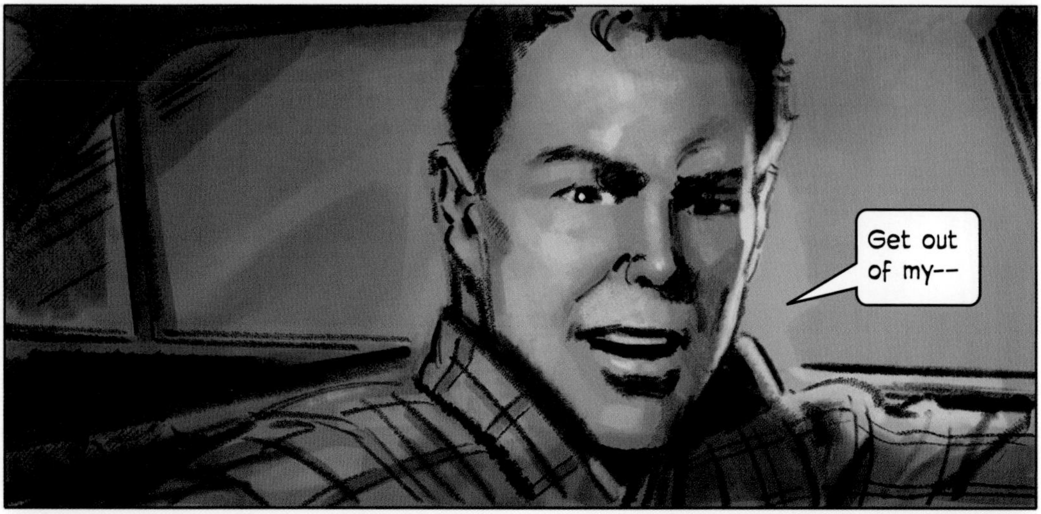
Get out of my--

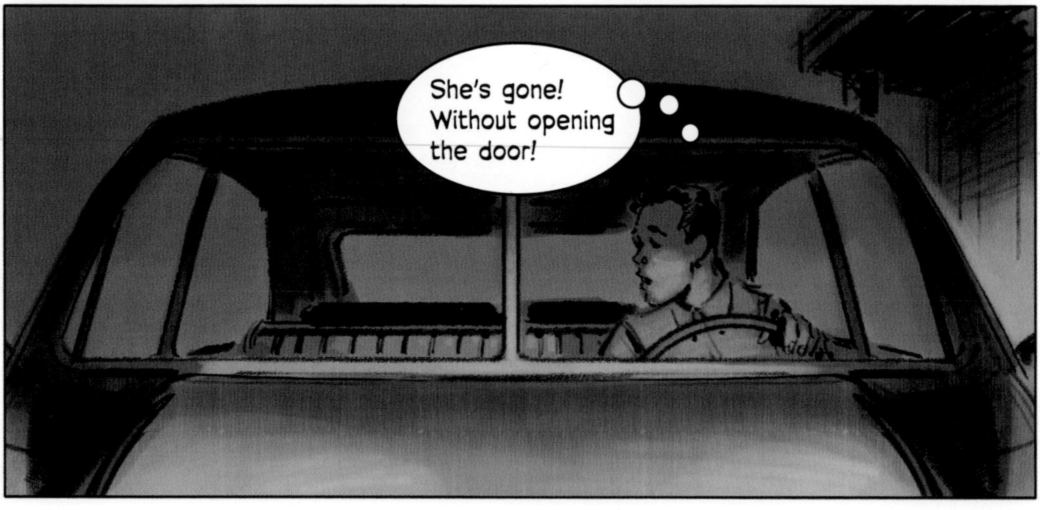
She's gone! Without opening the door!

A terrifying scream suddenly ripped through the air.

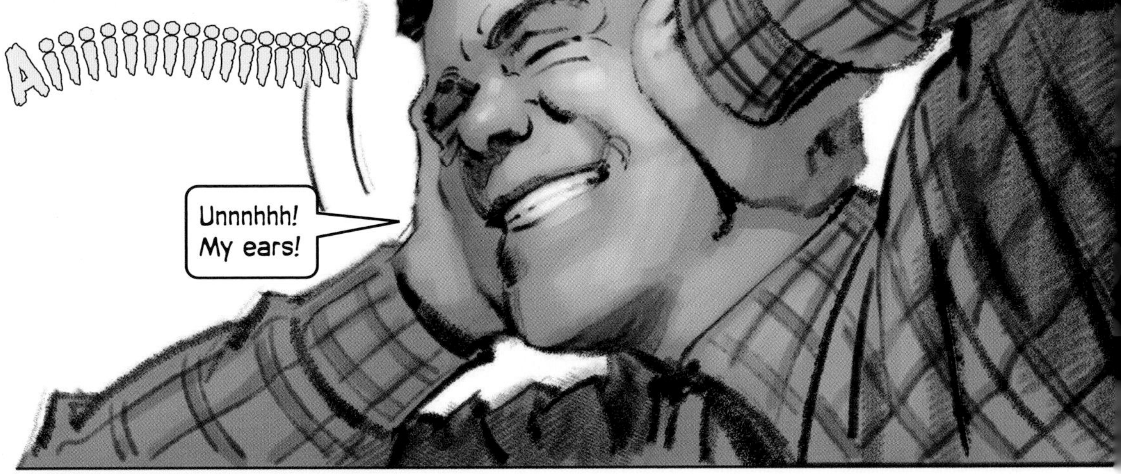
Aiiiiiiiiiiiiiiii
Unnnhhh! My ears!

Later, Ray finally arrived in La Joya.

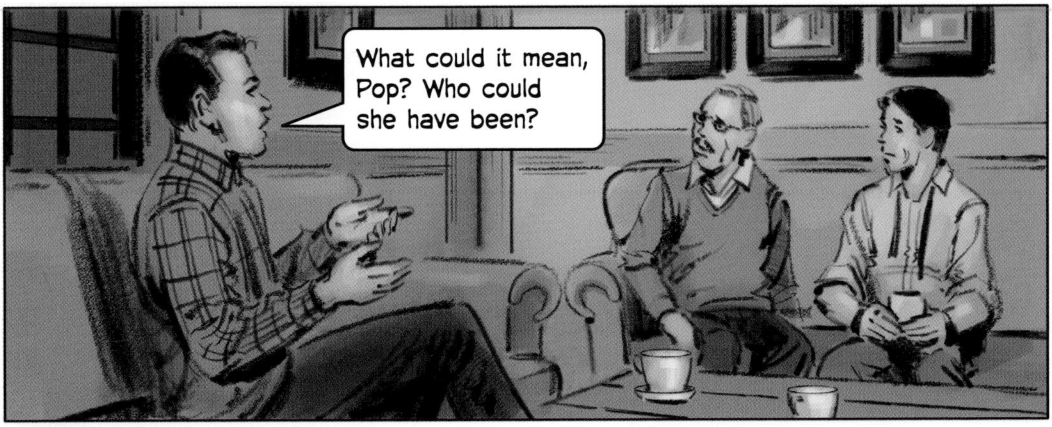
What could it mean, Pop? Who could she have been?

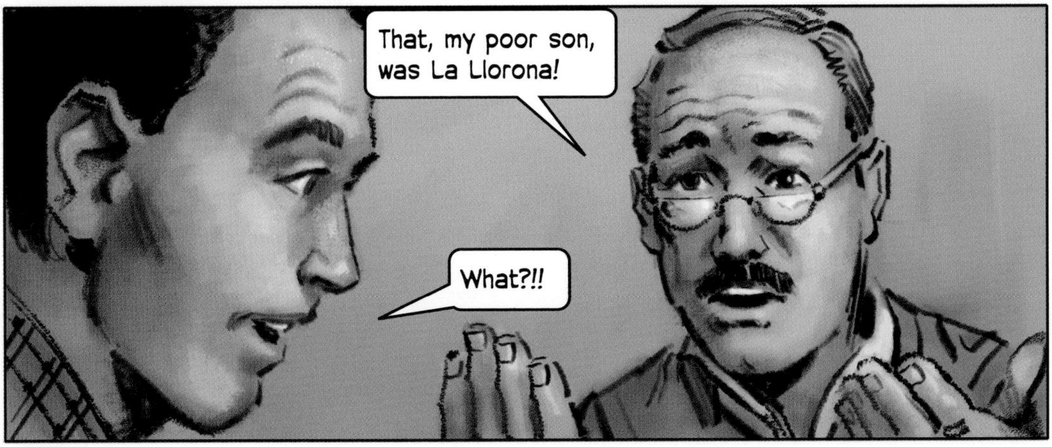
That, my poor son, was La Llorona!
What?!!

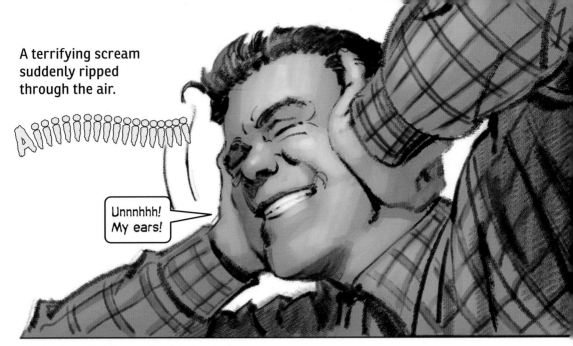

What does the legend of La Llorona mean and why has it lived on?

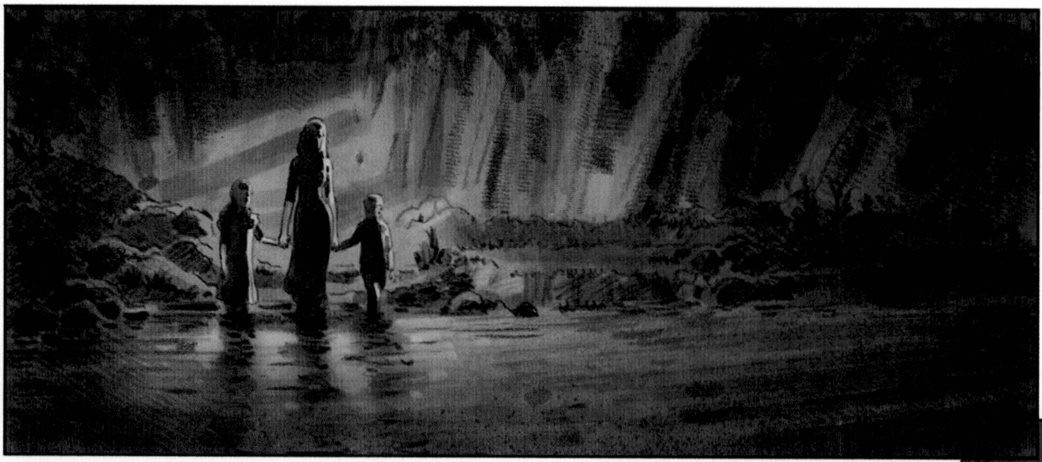

Many people believe the story was an omen of doom. They think La Llorona represented the Spanish taking over Aztec Mexico in the 16th century.

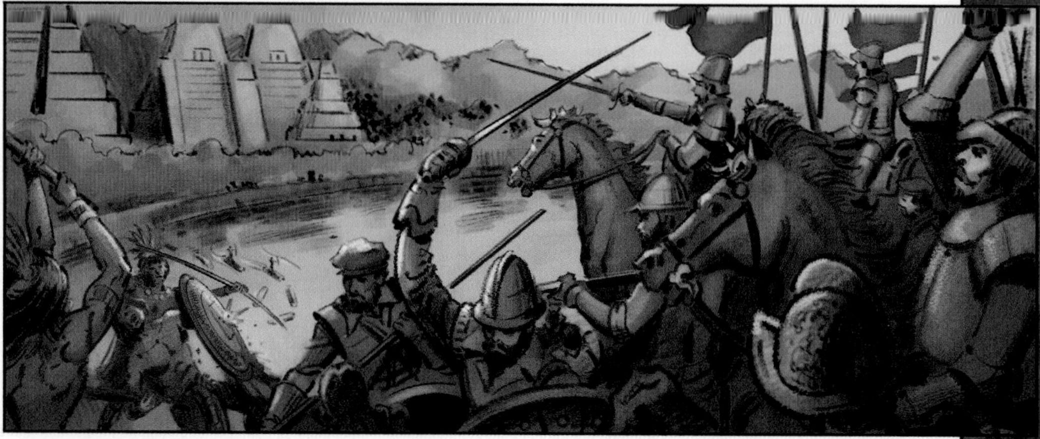

Others have used the tale to frighten young children.

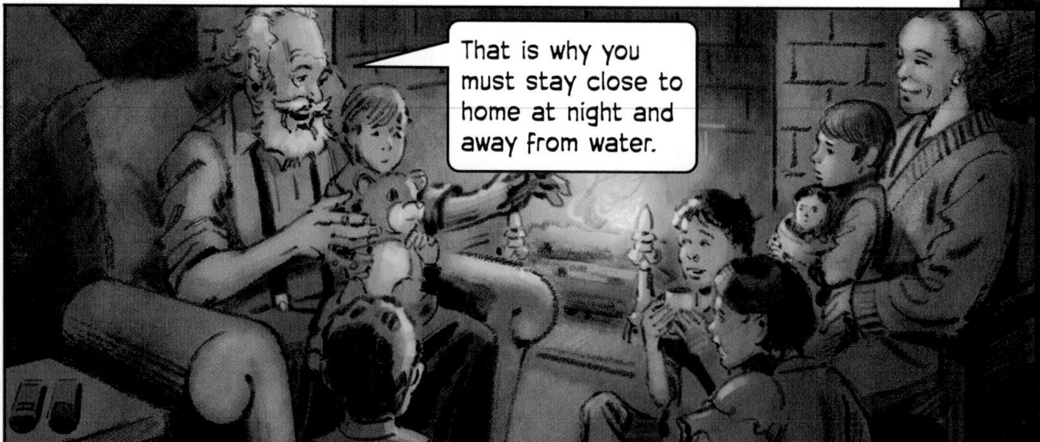
That is why you must stay close to home at night and away from water.

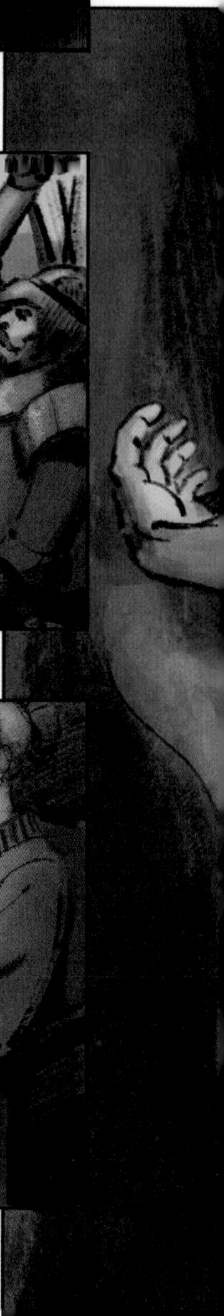

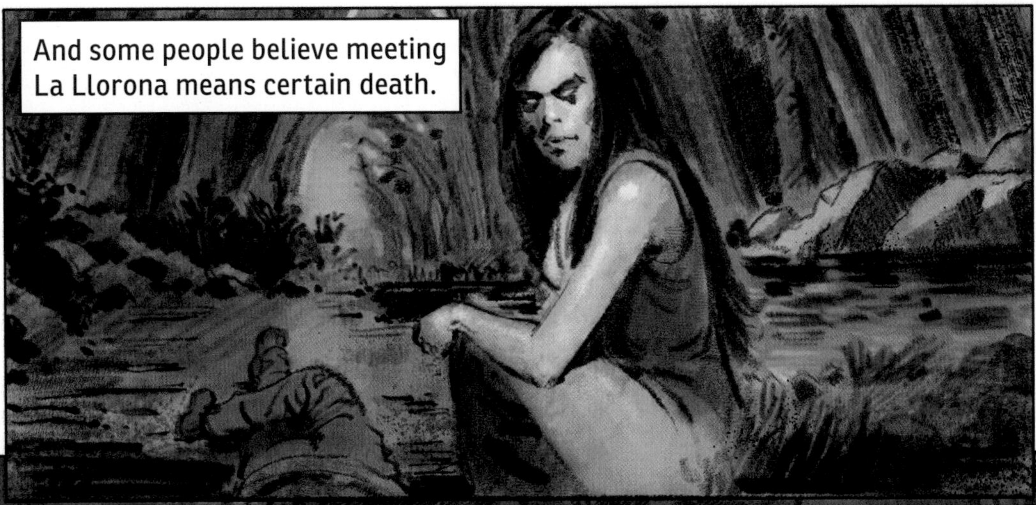
And some people believe meeting La Llorona means certain death.

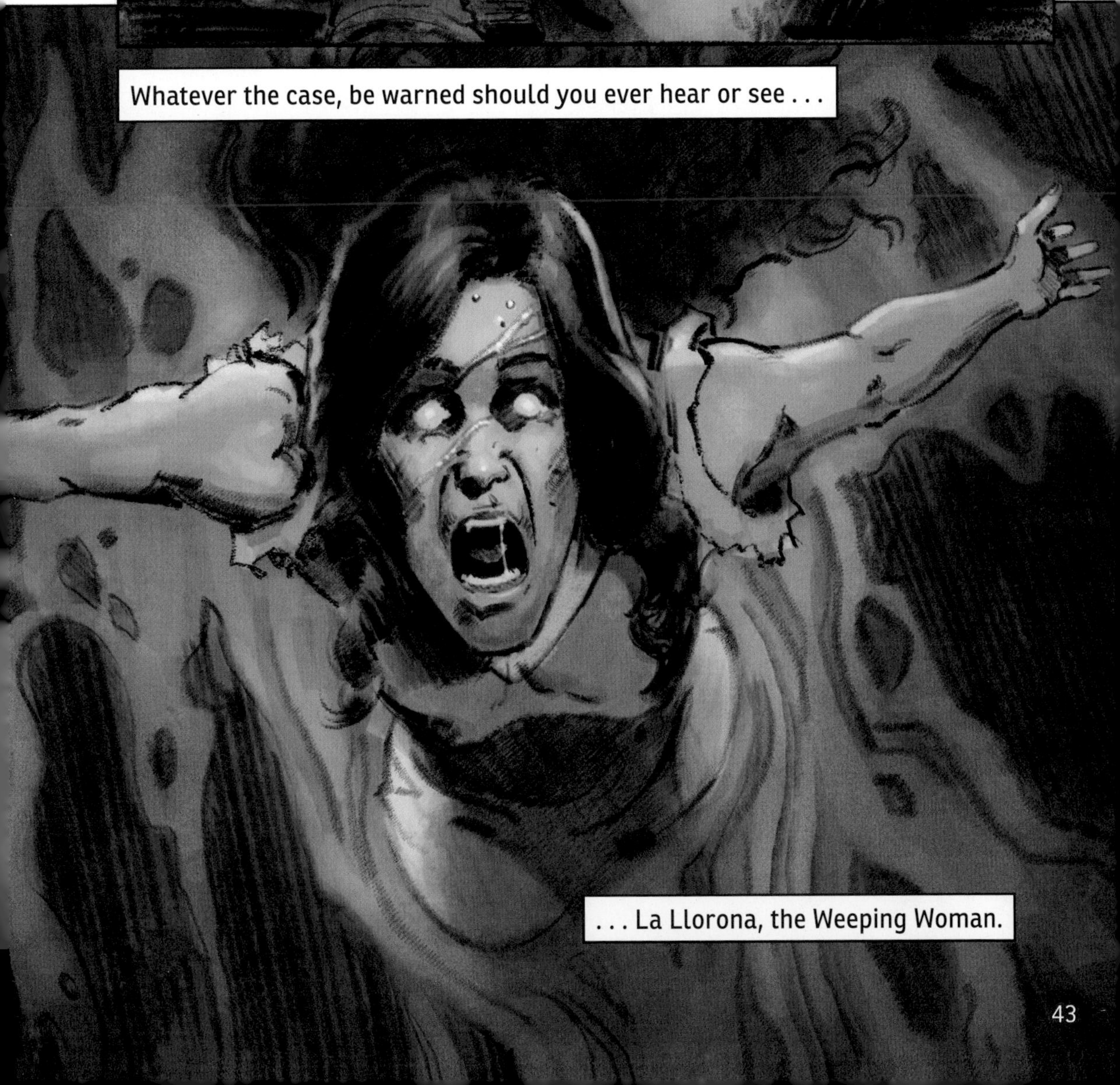
Whatever the case, be warned should you ever hear or see . . .
. . . La Llorona, the Weeping Woman.

MORE ABOUT LA LLORONA

- The Latin American story of La Llorona dates back to the 1500s. For many years, it was simply told and retold out loud. It wasn't written down until Manuel Carpio wrote the poem "La Llorona" in the 1800s.

- There are many versions of the La Llorona tale. Each one is a little different. In one version, she was not allowed to get into heaven. Instead, she must wander the earth as punishment for her crime.

- One popular version of the La Llorona tale is called "The Tragic Widow." In it, Maria is told her son has drowned in a flooding river. Every night after his death, she cries and wails along the banks of the river, "Ayyyyy miii hiiiijoooo! Where is my son?"

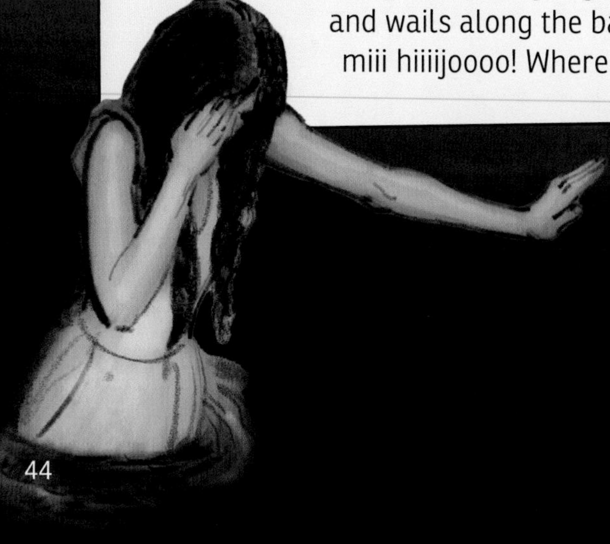

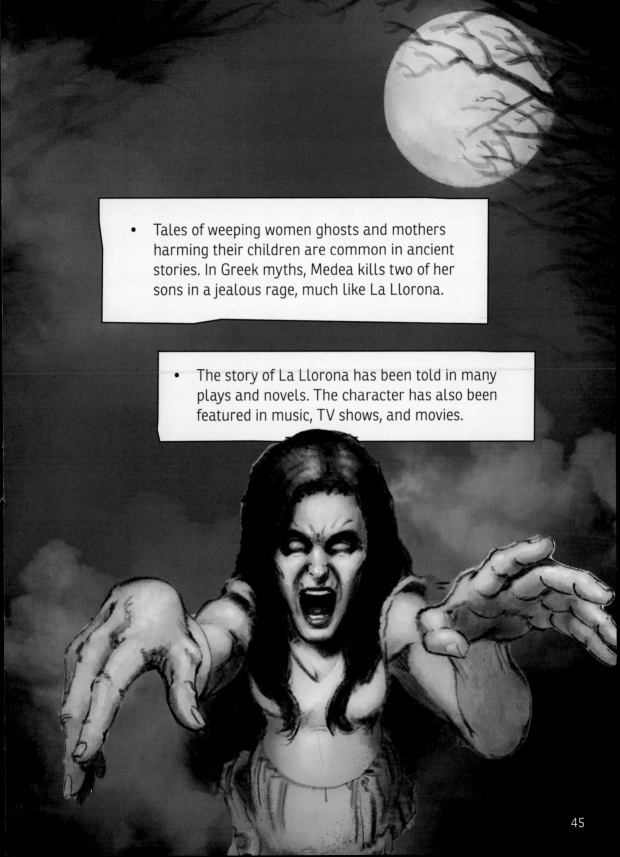

- Tales of weeping women ghosts and mothers harming their children are common in ancient stories. In Greek myths, Medea kills two of her sons in a jealous rage, much like La Llorona.

- The story of La Llorona has been told in many plays and novels. The character has also been featured in music, TV shows, and movies.

GLOSSARY

demon (DEE-muhn)—a devil, or an evil spirit

encounter (en-KOUN-tur)—an unexpected or difficult meeting

jealous (JEL-uhss)—wanting something someone else has

omen (OH-men)—a sign of something that will happen in the future

revenge (rih-VENJ)—an action taken to repay harm done

soul (SOLE)—the spiritual part of a person that is believed to live on after death

sulfur (SUHL-fur)—a yellow chemical that smells like rotten eggs

tombstone (TOOM-stone)—a carved block of stone that marks the place where someone is buried

town crier (TOUN KRY-uhr)—someone who makes public announcements in the streets or marketplace of a town

tradition (truh-DISH-uhn)—a custom, idea, or belief passed down through time

woe (WOH)—great sadness or grief

READ MORE

Katz, Susan B. *Famous Ghosts.* Minneapolis: Lerner Publications, 2024.

Peterson, Megan Cooley. *La Llorona: The Legendary Weeping Woman of Mexico.* North Mankato, MN: Capstone Press, 2020.

Troupe, Thomas Kingsley. *Searching for Ghosts.* Mankato, MN: Black Rabbit Books, 2021.

INTERNET SITES

Inside the Legend of La Llorona, the Vengeful Spirit of the Southwest
allthatsinteresting.com/la-llorona

La Llorona: A Mexican Ghost Story
donquijote.org/mexican-culture/history/la-llorona

Monstrum: The Legend of La Llorona
pbs.org/video/the-legend-of-la-llorona-gvx6ly

ABOUT THE AUTHOR

Photo by Nancy Golden

Nel Yomtov is an award-winning author of children's nonfiction books and graphic novels. He specializes in writing about history, current events, biography, architecture, and military history. He has written numerous graphic novels for Capstone, including the recent *School Strike for Climate*, *Journeying to New Worlds: A Max Axiom Super Scientist Adventure*, and *Cher Ami: Heroic Carrier Pigeon of World War I*. In 2020, he self-published *Baseball 100*, an illustrated book featuring the 100 greatest players in baseball history. Nel lives in the New York City area.

ABOUT THE ILLUSTRATOR

Photo by Richter Studio

Jason Millet has provided illustrations, storyboards and concept art for publishing, advertising, television, and films. His clients include NBC-Universal, Fox, Amblin Partners, HBO, Showtime, Disney, DC Comics, *The Wall Street Journal*, Scholastic Books, Wizards of the Coast, and Dark Horse Publishing among many others. Additionally, he has worked on ad campaigns for everything from Ford trucks to Happy Meals. He lives in Chicago with his wife, daughter, and very scary house cat.